Seven Days to
THE CROSS

By
Brian Byrne

TEACH Services, Inc.
P U B L I S H I N G
www.TEACHServices.com • (800) 367-1844

World rights reserved. This book or any portion thereof may not be copied or reproduced in any form or manner whatever, except as provided by law, without the written permission of the publisher, except by a reviewer who may quote brief passages in a review.

The author assumes full responsibility for the accuracy of all facts and quotations as cited in this book. The opinions expressed in this book are the author's personal views and interpretations, and do not necessarily reflect those of the publisher.

This book is provided with the understanding that the publisher is not engaged in giving spiritual, legal, medical, or other professional advice. If authoritative advice is needed, the reader should seek the counsel of a competent professional.

Copyright © 2014 Brian Byrne
Copyright © 2014 TEACH Services, Inc.
ISBN-13: 978-1-47960-255-1 (Paperback)
ISBN-13: 978-1-47960-256-8 (ePub)
ISBN-13: 978-1-47960-257-5 (Mobi)
Library of Congress Control Number: 2014900518

Published by

www.TEACHServices.com • (800) 367-1844

All scripture quotations, unless otherwise indicated, are taken from the New King James Version®. Copyright © 1982 by Thomas Nelson, Inc. Used by permission. All rights reserved.

Scripture quotations marked HCSB are taken from the Holman Christian Standard Bible®, Copyright © 1999, 2000, 2002, 2003, 2009 by Holman Bible Publishers. Used by permission.

Scripture quotations marked NIV are taken from the Holy Bible, New International Version®, NIV®. Copyright © 1973, 1978, 1984, 2011 by Biblica, Inc.™ Used by permission of Zondervan. All rights reserved worldwide.

Scripture quotations marked KJV are taken from the King James Version. Public domain.

Contents

Note from the Author 7

Introduction: Lighthouse Over Time 9

FRIDAY: We Are Going Up to Jerusalem 15

SATURDAY: They Made Him a Supper................................ 19

SUNDAY: Behold Your King Comes.................................... 21

MONDAY: You Have Made It a Den of Thieves 25

TUESDAY: You Shall Love the Lord Your God................... 31

TUESDAY: Whitewashed Tombs.. 40

TUESDAY EVENING: When Shall These Things Be? 55

WEDNESDAY: Your Father, the Devil 59

THURSDAY: I Have Desired to Eat This Passover 67

THURSDAY: I Will Not Leave You Orphans...................... 75

THURSDAY NIGHT: The Hour Has Come........................... 85

THURSDAY NIGHT and FRIDAY MORNING:

    They All Forsook Him 94

FRIDAY: The Cross 103

SUNDAY: He Is Risen 116

EPILOGUE: Take Up Your Cross... 125

Note from **the Author**

The cross is the foundation of all I believe. Without it, my salvation is derelict, and I am deprived of the power to make a difference in my own life and, consequently, in the life of others. The cross is so much more than a doctrine or a set of encapsulated teachings. Paul made this clear when he wrote that "the message of the cross is foolishness to those who are perishing, but to us who are being saved it is the power of God" (1 Cor. 1:18).

I have to take Paul seriously, for it would be foolishness to lock up the message of the cross in the closet of my mind and deny myself access to its power. But how do I discover the power of that central element in my faith? Books won't do it. What I learn at church may touch the fringes of the power of the cross, but I long for more than that. I want to have all the principles of the cross deeply and firmly embedded in my mind and heart, and to do that I have to walk the path our Savior walked from Jericho to Golgotha. That is the motivation that has brought this book into being.

There is a common misunderstanding afloat in the waters of church life. It is the idea that once I have come to the Lord carrying my heart's repentance in both hands, confessed to Him all my wrong doings, and received His forgiveness, only then will I enter the kingdom of God Jesus referred to with Nicodemus. This is all true, but it is only a small truth opening the door to a much larger truth that Jesus spelled out. If I am to be His disciple I will need to learn how to take up my cross daily and follow Him (see Luke 9:23).

Those words are powerful enough, but the Lord added another principle that puts those words in the context of His approval. He made it clear to His disciples that taking up their cross was the only way they could be worthy of Him (see Matt. 10:38).

I have a choice, but if I am to accept the fact that I want and need His approval in order to be worthy of Him, I do not really have a choice after all. I must deny myself, take up my cross daily, and follow Him. But then I am faced with the question: where do I find the pattern that reveals how I am to take up my cross?

The Lord had anticipated my question. He told His disciples who had left everything to follow Him that every disciple needed to pattern their life after their teacher (see Matt. 10:25). He is the pattern, for He took up His own cross and walked where the Father directed, from the palace of Pontius Pilate to Golgotha where He gave up His life. And so I now must follow in His footsteps. I must listen and learn about how the message of His cross can add power to my own life.

There will be three benefits for me as I write this narrative. I will understand more completely what He suffered that day and be better able to teach others about the central Person in our faith. That will be the first benefit. The second benefit for me in writing this narrative is that I will add so much more to my own understanding of myself in my walk with Him as His disciple and servant.

For that understanding to take root and flourish, I have to open my heart to the gentle and yet insistent voice of my Teacher, who is the Spirit of truth. I don't seek doctrine. I have that in abundance. Instead, I seek His revelation of the principles of the cross, which are to be matched precisely, as only He knows how, with the often tentative state of my inner being.

The third benefit will come as I am guided to seek and find the principles that underpin what it means to carry my own cross. Those principles will all be there for me as they were for Him. The Father set these principles in place, and they applied to His Son as to my Elder Brother and to me (see Rom. 8:29).

I will tell the story of the cross in a number of chapters that match the progress of my Lord from Jericho to Golgotha, and these will be arranged in a daily sequence, from the Friday when He left Jericho to the following Friday when He was crucified.

The account of what I will learn about myself will be told in footnotes to each chapter arranged under the heading "In His Footsteps." These are personal, but I will share them with you, for there may be insights into your own walk with the Master that resonate with your spirit, as you deny yourself, daily take up your own cross, and follow Him.

In writing these notes, I have taken a liberty for which I ask your forgiveness. I have written as though I was present at each of the events on those seven days and on the following Sunday. This artifice has enabled me to engage more closely with the truth of those days and with the principles that underpinned them. Only as I wrote of those events as a close observer could I escape the trap of reading the Scriptures as merely doctrine and not as the living accounts of real people.

The principles of what it means to take up my own cross and follow Him will be explored in the epilogue, "Take Up Your Cross." There are seven of these principles. In the first six, I will explore the changes needed in my own heart's attitudes as I apply what He Himself experienced on that walk from Jericho to Golgotha. In the seventh principle, I will explore the outward look into the world of the lost where the power of the message of the cross may be displayed.

There is only one thing to add and that is a word of counsel. As you engage in your own journey from Jericho to Golgotha, you may, if you seek His presence and counsel, enjoy the presence of the Comforter, the Spirit of the Father, who has been called to walk beside you on your own journey to the cross. His presence will be of inestimable benefit because, according to Jesus' own promise, He will interpret all that you see and hear and imprint it on your heart with His own gentle touch, thus training you in the ways of the kingdom and equipping you to take up your own cross and follow Him.

Introduction
Lighthouse Over Time

The cross stands over time like a lighthouse in the midst of a turbulent sea. The waves of human argument and dissent beat against it but can never overwhelm it. Its light pierces the darkness for that is the reason it stands there above humankind, above history, and above time itself. And that is the purpose our God has given to the cross, to be a light in the darkness, a tower where humanity may find refuge. It represents the ultimate in suffering, which no one may ever comprehend, for it is certainly the kind of suffering that we may never experience.

What is the connection, I ask, between all the forms the cross takes in church and chapel, on printed page, in symbol, and action as well as the events on Golgotha nearly twenty centuries ago? Is there a connection at all? Or has humankind turned its understanding of a death filled with unspeakable horror into something they could deal with without having to enter that horror? Like turning the unspeakable into a prosaic and even mundane artifact of religion or of no religion at all?

Come over the hill with me.
I want to show you where the cross stood
beside Jerusalem.
It is a long way there,
and I don't think we have the time.
The hill deceives, doesn't it?
A steep thing, strong on the south side,
and ascending rapidly to a broken arch
built by Constantine.
Time is too short to go all the way.
See how the brickwork is jointed
and there is a cross carved high on the lintel.
We need go no farther.

I have decided to go beyond the cross that is carved high on the lintel and leave behind the artifacts of religion. I want to turn instead to the One who died there only to rise again. My search has to be focused on the only One who can lead me into all truth, as the Lord Himself promised, for He is the Spirit of truth. He is also the Spirit of the One who died that day and the Spirit of the Father who sent His Only Begotten Son to die between two thieves.

But why search? Is it not better to accept what humankind had said and written about the cross and walk in the light of great traditions that have been left in our wake? For many, that is enough, but I am confronted by the Lord's own words directing me, and so many like me, to His words about denying myself and taking up my cross daily (see Matt. 16:24). And how can I obey such an instruction if I have no knowledge of what the cross meant to the One who died there?

Many have made light of these words and translated the Lord's injunction into a prosaic platitude. In many circles both within the church and out of it, it is said that every person has a cross to bear. And in those words, people divest the cross of its awful and cruel majesty and make it akin to something human that we all must put up with: our neighbor, who constantly throws his rubbish over our fence, or a government imposition that we have trouble paying, or an in-law, who constantly refuses to recognize our son's birthday. Such lists are endless and all attempt to give substance to the words "We all have our cross to bear." But those platitudes give terrible slight to the bleeding Son of Man bearing His cross to death, almost amounting to blasphemy. I deny all these attempts to humanize what can only be divine and will be guided in my search by the truth of what happened that day so long ago. This is the intent of my search.

There is only one source of any value in my search: the inspired pages of the Sacred Scriptures. There I find first hand accounts of one who was there at that time (John), of one who was close by but fled from its horrors (Matthew), by two others whose research provided them with details of what happened that day on Golgotha (Mark and Luke), and another (Paul) who learned what the cross meant through the personal revelation of its mysteries by the Spirit of the One who died there.

The story of the cross did not begin when the Jewish leaders conspired to have Jesus put to death. Nor did it begin when Isaiah transcribed the Lord's inspired words now recorded in his fifty-third chapter, which was written more than 600 years before the Savior's death. The story of the cross is much older than that. There was an event predictive of the cross that happened in the sands of northern Egypt more than 1,400 years before the Messiah was born. A lamb was slain, and its blood splashed on the doorposts and lintel of the front door of every Jewish home. God's purpose was to give the angel of death a sign that he was to pass over that house and be diverted from his assigned task: to kill all the firstborn sons living in Egypt.

But the story of the cross is much older even than that. In the Garden of Eden, another event took place that was also predictive of the cross. The first couple, having eaten the forbidden fruit, found that they were naked and ashamed, and in fear, they hid in the darkness of the garden. The Lord, in His mercy, killed an animal, probably one each, and used the skins to fashion some kind of garment to cover their nakedness. This was a long-ago death to cover shame that we can now see was predictive of another death on a cross so that your shame and mine could be destroyed forever.

But the story of the cross has no beginning, for it was recorded in times beyond time that our minds cannot comprehend. The apostle John, writing as his Lord directed on the Island of Patmos during his exile, referred to the Lamb who had been slain from the foundation of the world (see Rev. 13:8). When the Father spoke the words that brought all the worlds into being, the plan had already been made. If our world fell, Jesus would carry His cross to Golgotha. There they would nail His hands and feet to that cross, and there He would die.

The time of that event is like an anvil on which the histories of humankind have been beaten into shape. It was like a pivoting hinge separating humankind of their sins, iniquities, and disobedience, from their future, where those the Father calls will become members of the kingdom He will come to rule.

This book is about the cross as the Scriptures depict that event. In order to best search to understand the cross, I have to delve into the words the Father dictated across the history of His own people. Those words let us into two mysteries. The cross was the place where two strands of Jewish history came together: the mystery of the kingship of the Messiah and the parallel mystery of His suffering. One noble and set to rule while the other ignoble and given to suffering.

The history of the people of God always involved the Father's desire that His people be gathered into a nation, and that He rule that nation through His own laws and the administration of His own justice. The purpose was noble. The fulfillment of that purpose was marred because of people ruled by the evil intentions and impulses they inherited out of Eden. They were captive to an old nature where sin ruled unto death.

Jeremiah spoke time and again of the Father's frustration with those that created conflict with God's plan for His own people. The words the Father gave to Moses so many years before found continual expression in Adam's descendants across the centuries. "Then the Lord saw that the wickedness of man was great on the earth, and that every intent of the thoughts of his heart was only evil continually" (Gen. 6:5).

The Lord God had two serious problems in those dark centuries before Christ: the sins of His own people and the death that accompanied their sin. Paul tied these two issues into one image when he wrote that the wages of sin was death (see Rom. 6:23). Both had to be dealt with for humanity to be truly free.

But there was another failure in the life of God's people. Kingship had failed, and it did so because all kings were cursed with the same plight of the common man. They had also inherited the sinful nature out of Eden and expressed that nature in the evil they did in the sight of the Lord (see 2 Chron. 22:4; 33:22).

Tied to the failure of these kings to rule justly was another connection. All the kings of the single kingdom of Israel, and later of the divided kingdoms of Judah and Israel, whether they were anointed by the Father or put on their thrones by man, from Saul to Zedekiah, they were each tied by their sins to the sins of the people. Their own sins became the prism through which they had to watch over the people they ruled. This had always been the case, but the Messiah needed to break this connection. He had to be of the people yet not tied to them by sharing their sinful nature.

There were two massive problems among the people on whom the Lord had vested His name: the sin living within that so easily beset them and the need for the rule of a just king so that His people might be brought under the covering of His law and justice. The Messiah would have to deal with both.

But the prophecies of the Messiah reveal two surprising elements in the Father's plans. He would both rule and suffer. His kingship over the Lord's people, Israel, appears in a variety of prophecies from Isaiah to Zechariah. Isaiah wrote, "For unto us [the people of Israel] a Child is born, unto us a Son is given; and the government [of the people of Israel] will be upon His shoulder, and His name will be called Wonderful, Counselor, Mighty God, Everlasting Father, Prince of Peace" (Isa. 9:6). Micah was more specific in his prophecy of the Messiah when he wrote that the One who was eternal and would be the Ruler of Israel would come out of Bethlehem (see Mic. 5:2).

These promises and so many like them would have been in the minds of the disciples when they stood with the Lord on the Mount of Olives and asked the Lord whether He would at that time restore the kingdom to Israel (see Acts 1:6). Like so many of their people they had a single-minded attitude about the coming of the Messiah. He would come to rule over His own people.

It is important to note that prophecies of the coming Messiah were first directed to the people of Israel, the descendants of Abraham, and not to those who would later become part of the Lord's *ekklesia* (church). The wonderful truths embedded in these prophecies have been applied to ourselves by so many Christians, but we have to admit that they were not directed primarily to us but to the Lord's own Jewish people, and that makes His rejection by the same people all the more surprising.

The other aspect of the Messiah's life and of the Father's purposes seems like a contradiction, for it stands in such appalling opposition to His royalty. It is about His suffering and subsequent death. Isaiah wrote, "But He was wounded for our transgressions, He was bruised for our iniquities; the chastisement for our peace was upon Him, and by His stripes we are healed" (Isa. 53:5). Isaiah had no foreknowledge or forethought of the coming church of God, and the personal pronouns "our" and "we" in this prophecy initially related to Israel. Daniel was very specific when he wrote that the Messiah would be cut off for humanity (see Dan. 9:26).

Our final prophecy of the suffering Messiah comes from the inspired pen of Zechariah, pointing to a time in the far distance when God will indeed restore the kingdom to the house of David. Zechariah wrote, "And I will pour on the house of David and on the inhabitants of Jerusalem the Spirit of grace and supplication; then they will look on Me whom they pierced. Yes, they will mourn for Him as one mourns for his only son, and grieve for Him as one grieves for a firstborn" (Zech. 12:10).

These two strands of prophecy are eternally bound together: the One who will rule with the One whose rule was founded on His suffering. And in the final book of our Scriptures, these two strands of prophecy are bound together into an image both beautiful and strongly compelling. I give the words John the prophet wrote the significance they deserve.

> *Now I saw heaven opened, and behold, a white horse. And He who sat on him was called Faithful and True, and in righteousness He judges and makes war. His eyes were like a flame of fire, and on His head were many crowns. He had a name written that no one knew except Himself. He was clothed with a robe dipped in blood, and His name is called The Word of God.* (Rev. 19:11–13)

In these words the prophecies of the suffering Messiah and of the royal King, which were first directed to Israel, now encompass the whole world. First Israel, then the church of Jesus Christ is added, and then the whole of humankind becomes the environment in which He will rule. And to accomplish that eternal plan the Father had to send His Son to die.

This following narrative will begin with the day Jesus and His disciples climbed through the hills and gorges from Jericho to Jerusalem. It will include descriptions of what happened during the last seven days of His earthly life. In this narrative we will explore the lives and responses of those who were there and delve as deeply as His Spirit allows into the mind and purposes of the Father, who set all those events in motion. Our search will end when we explore the Lord's instruction to take up the cross, on which we have also been crucified, and follow Him.

To use a modern idiom, this could be a bumpy ride. Old stereotypes about the cross may have to be re-examined in the light of what the Scriptures teach. Superficial doctrines might have to give way to the deeper truths of the cross. And the ways of life we have come to be associated with our religion might have to be challenged as we obey His own words to deny ourselves and take up our cross and follow Him (see Luke 9:23).

Chapter One
FRIDAY: We Are Going Up to Jerusalem

Introduction

It was the day before the Sabbath and Jesus and His disciples were in Jericho. It was there that the Lord had met and forgiven Zacchaeus, the errant tax collector. Jesus had then dined with him and with his fellow tax collectors. The next morning as He was leaving Jericho, He encountered Bartimaeus, the blind beggar, whom He healed before leaving to go to His beloved city, the place where He would die.

The day that Jesus left Jericho for the final walk into the hills of Judea was the day before the Sabbath. According to Jewish custom, the Sabbath began at sunset when the first three stars appeared in the evening sky and ended twenty-four hours later with sunset and the appearance of the same stars. He and His disciples had to arrive in Bethany before the Sabbath began.

For the Lord and His disciples, the events of that Sabbath are split into two parts: those that took place on the evening of Friday after Jesus and His disciples arrived from Jericho, and those that took place the following day, Saturday, the continuation of the Sabbath.

The scriptural basis for dating these events is provided by Matthew, Mark, and John. Luke is silent about what happened in Bethany. Matthew and Mark tell us that Jesus spent some time in the home of the person known as Simon the leper (see Matt. 26:6; Mark 14:3). The fact that this was his name strongly suggests that he had been healed by the Lord and therefore wished to give a dinner in Jesus' honor. Mark places these events two days before Passover (see Mark 14:1–3) while John places them four days earlier, making a total of six days before Passover (see John 12:1).

I cannot rationalize this discrepancy and have decided to rely on the noted biblical scholar, Alfred Edersheim, who was a Jewish convert to Christianity. His noted work, *The Life and Times of Jesus the Messiah*, is recommended reading for all serious students of the life of our Lord.

Edersheim places the dinner in the home of Simon the leper, and he says that the events that involved Mary took place on the Saturday after the Lord's arrival from Jericho. The date is unimportant. The details are vital to our understanding of Jesus' walk to the cross.

Walk to Jerusalem

The Lord began His final walk to the cross from Jericho. This was not the ancient Jericho where the prostitute Rahab protected the two spies sent by Joshua from discovery, or where the infamous Achan stole the Babylonian garment, the wedge of gold and the silver. That Jericho was a relic of Joshua's past and was being steadily covered by the sands of the surrounding desert.

Herod the Great had built the new Jericho on both sides of the Wadi Qelt. It became his winter palace, and it was famous for its reflecting pools, marble staircases lined with statuary, and its sunken gardens. Once Herod had died, the buildings were burned down by disaffected citizens rebelling about his previous rule. Herod's son, Archelaus, restored the town. It became the center for tax collecting in the region, which is most likely why it was the home of the tax collector Zacchaeus.

When Jesus left Jericho, He knew what awaited Him after His long climb to Jerusalem. Just before He came to Jericho He took His disciples aside and told them:

Behold, we are going up to Jerusalem, and all things that are written by the prophets concerning the Son of Man will be accomplished. For He will be delivered to the Gentiles and will be mocked and insulted and spit upon. They will scourge Him and kill Him. And the third day He will rise again. (Luke 18:31–33)

This was the third occasion when the Lord told them of His coming death (see Mark 8:31; 9:31).

It was Friday, the day before the Sabbath, when Jesus and His disciples left the city of palms and crossed the Wadi Qelt. They had to be in Jerusalem before sunset after which no travel was permitted for practicing Jews. From the narrow plain along the Jordan, they began the climb into the hills of Judea. They passed under the shelter of the 500-foot cliff face, pierced by caverns where hermits live today, but they were the dwelling places of robbers and thieves in Jesus' day (see Luke 10:30). Their path led them across the lip of the tremendous gorge of the Wadi Qelt, and as they looked down into its depths, they could see strips of vegetation and agricultural plantings.

From there their path led through numerous steep valleys where winter torrents had raked the stones bare. And finally, they came to the rocky natural staircase that served as a road leading them to the ascent of the Mount of Olives. There the path divided. One path led across the Mount of Olives to Jerusalem, and the other led into the hamlet of Bethany.

Bethany

The Lord knew the hamlet of Bethany well. It was a place of welcome and rest after the six-hour climb from Jericho to Jerusalem. Lazarus, whom He had raised from the dead, along with his two sisters, Martha and Mary, welcomed Him and His disciples into the home they had prepared for their Sabbath celebrations. This was to be our Lord's base for the remaining days of His life among them. And, as we shall see, Mary knew that the Lord had come for His death.

Martha and Mary carefully prepared dishes of vegetables, bread, meat, fish, and poultry; there were multiple dishes because the Sabbath was a festive occasion. The house was thoroughly cleaned. Lazarus and his guests washed and dressed in their best clothes before the Sabbath meal.

According to custom the Sabbath candles were lit eighteen minutes before sunset. This was followed by the traditional statement welcoming in the Sabbath service. Martha, Mary, Lazarus, and their guests then sang a special hymn and after the ritual washing of hands, they sat down (more like reclined) for the Sabbath meal. Selected words from the Torah (the five books of Moses) were read during the meal, and the evening concluded with the ritual blessing. As the age-old custom dictated, the Sabbath had now officially begun, and they all retired for the night.

In His Footsteps

I began the walk to Golgotha at Jericho in the company of another who had also been born blind. Like me, he had remained so until the day he encountered the Lord and there been healed. I also was born blind. Not the outer blindness of my companion but the inner blindness of eyes that resisted the light and would not see. But once I met the Lord, my inner eyes were opened, and for the first time, I could see.

I began the walk to Jerusalem also in the company of One whom I hardly knew. Much has been written about Him, but the recognition of His continuing mercies and compassion was, at times, elusive and unattainable for me. I had indeed encountered His mercies while I was yet in my exuberant and recalcitrant teenage years, but many more years were to pass before I would begin to understand who He truly was.

On this walk to Golgotha, I had committed myself to learn much more about the Lord as He faced into the final days and hours of His earthly life. He had been sent by the Father to save the world, including myself, from the awful pedigrees of sin we had all inherited from generations before us.

As I began this journey to the cross, I trusted that I would also gain more of the sobering knowledge of who I truly am. He walked ahead of me; I followed in His footsteps. Slowly but surely, as we climbed into the hills of Judea, I came to see that soon the way to Golgotha would be closed to Him forever.

Chapter Two
SATURDAY: They Made Him a Supper

The Home in Bethany

The Sabbath was passed in quiet activities. Again, there are very few details, but we know that work was not permitted and meals could not be cooked until after the three stars appeared in the evening sky. The only walking that was permitted was a Sabbath day's journey, limited to a thousand double paces.

The time was usually spent in reflection and quiet conversation in and around the home. During this special time, I believe Mary sat at the feet of the One she loved and whom she knew would soon die (see Luke 10:38–42).

The House of Simon the Leper

In Matthew's account of the dinner given in Jesus' honor, two strands of our story come together: the understanding that Jesus had been told by the Father that He was going to die the horrifying death of crucifixion and Mary's knowledge that His death was imminent. The dinner in the home of Simon the leper was in progress with Martha serving and Lazarus reclining at the table with the Lord.

However, the meal was interrupted when Mary brought her most precious possession: an alabaster flask of oil of spikenard worth 300 dinars into the room where they reclined. It was worth the equivalent of a man' wages for one year and was capable of feeding 3500 men and their families. Unashamed, Mary knelt behind her Lord and poured the precious ointment on His feet.

It is possible that Mary had purchased the spikenard some time previously and had kept it perhaps for the time when she would marry, but as the time of Jesus' death drew near, she understood that her time with her Lord was coming to an end, so she took the precious oil into the dining room. There she anointed her Lord, and perhaps while weeping, she let down her hair and wiped away the oil from His feet with her hair.

We must pass over the unworthy comments of Judas, for they draw our attention away from one of the most beautiful acts of any woman towards our Lord. Instead we note His own words in which He immortalized her love for Him. "For in pouring this fragrant oil on My body, she did it for My burial. Assuredly, I say to you, wherever this gospel is preached in the whole world, what this woman has done will also be told as a memorial to her" (Matt. 26:12, 13).

Jesus knew Mary so well. He knew her love and her quiet single-hearted devotion, and He acknowledged that she knew His death was looming. In that simple act, her bond with her Lord forged a love for Him and His acceptance of her gift that would never be destroyed. No tears are recorded, but Mary would have gone home that night knowing that she understood a small part of the last days of the life of the One she loved, and that He knew she knew and understood Him as few others ever would.

So, we come to end of that Saturday. All retired for the night, with Jesus secure in knowing that a prophecy made in Babylon more than 600 years earlier would be fulfilled the next day when He entered Jerusalem.

In His Footsteps

What could I offer Him as I knelt at His feet at the table in the Pharisee's house? What do I possess that would be considered precious enough to use when I, like Mary, came to understand that He would die? I have only one possession that is mine to give. And every other thing I possess pales into insignificance beside this one gift I am able to offer Him. It is my own life.

The Scriptures have taught me the value of that gift, for Jesus spoke of it when He told His disciples if anyone wanted to save his life he would have to be prepared to lose it for Christ's sake (see Matt. 10:39). The question everyone faced in that dining room was: am I prepared to pour out my life at His feet as the ultimate love offering for the One who would soon pour out His own life unto death? I would find out my answer on this journey.

But I learned something else about this relationship with my Lord that night in the Pharisee's house. Although Mary knelt on the floor behind Him, He knew exactly what she had done. And when I also honor Him with the gift of the life I alone can bring Him, He will surely know who I am and what I have done.

When I give the Lord my life, there will be an exchange. I will lose my life, but He will surely give it back. Except that now it will be altered and enhanced and augmented with His Spirit, which will be interwoven with mine. I will find my life, but it will no longer be mine. Instead, it will be hidden in the life of the eternal Son of God.

Chapter Three
SUNDAY: Behold Your King Comes

The Crowds

Sunday dawned quietly in Bethany after the meal at the home of Simon the leper. At that time Jerusalem and the surrounding villages were crowded with many Jews from around the Roman Empire visiting the City of David for the Passover. Jews had a tradition of hospitality. Visitors were always welcome in every home, however rich or humble, and meals were always available.

In addition to those who were in Bethany for the Passover, there were also those who had come hoping to see Lazarus, for he had been raised from the dead, and this was a most unusual occurrence. It was a notable miracle and drew a great deal of interest. And the news that Jesus, about whom there were so many stories and rumors, was also in Bethany added to the crowd's interest.

This expanded population fell into two groups. There were those who lived in Jerusalem and who supported the violent future the Jewish leaders had for Jesus. The other crowd, those from the far-flung reaches of the empire, had no such expectations. While the first group would soon cry for Barabbas to be released instead of Jesus (see Mark 15:6–8), the gentler, openhearted group had not been part of the hysteria that had enveloped Jerusalem. They had simply been attracted by the rumors about Jesus and wanted to see the One who had performed so many miracles. Many of these people who had come to Bethany to see Jesus augmented the crowds that had come to see Lazarus. And when Jesus and His disciples left the house of Mary and Martha to go to Jerusalem, this crowd attached itself to them.

A large number of visitors for the Passover had lodged in the city and when news reached them that Jesus and His disciples had left Bethany and were coming to the City of David, they flocked out of the city gates to meet the Lord.

All the Jews at that time looked for the Messiah, for He was a central part of their belief system. The Messiah was tied inextricably to the kingdom they expected God to establish in Israel with the Messiah as its King. And these two ideas, kingdom and the Messiah, converged that day on the Lord's walk to Jerusalem.

The Foal of a Donkey

Early that Sunday morning, the Lord and His disciples left the house in Bethany and began the walk to the Holy City, which was hidden behind the Mount of Olives. Two disciples, perhaps Peter and John, were sent ahead to find and bring back the foal of an ass tied by the side of the road at Bethphage. When they did this, Jesus mounted the foal and turned its head towards the city.

At this point two crowds met and merged. The pilgrim crowd accompanying Him from Bethany and the crowd coming out of Jerusalem to see the One they knew as Jesus of Nazareth were united. They placed their cloaks on the foal and seated Jesus on its back. They broke branches from the trees, plaited mats, and spread them across the way on which their King would come. Then they began to chant in words taken from Psalm 118. "Hosanna! 'Blessed is He who comes in the name of the Lord!' The King of Israel!" (John 12:13).

This is the one and only time in the accounts of Jesus that He was referred to in public by the people as "the King of Israel." Two prophecies were fulfilled that day. The first is from the prophet Zechariah. "Rejoice greatly, O daughter of Zion! Shout in triumph, O daughter of Jerusalem! Behold, your king is coming to you; He is just and endowed with salvation, humble, and mounted on a donkey, even on a colt, the foal of a donkey" (Zech. 9:9, NASB).

The second prophecy is from Daniel who predicted that a period of sixty-nine weeks would elapse between the decree to rebuild the city of Jerusalem and the coming of the Messiah (see Dan. 9:25). The period Daniel prophesied about was fulfilled when Artaxerxes I Longimanus issued the first decree authorizing the Jews in Jerusalem to begin rebuilding the city "in troublous times" and provide for the complete restoration of the Jewish state and enforcement of its national laws. Daniel 9:25 is the only prophecy that specifies the time when the Messiah would appear.

As the stranger/pilgrim crowd followed Jesus on the foal of a donkey around one of the ridges on the slopes of the Mount of Olives, they caught their first sight of the Holy City. The eastern part of the city rose terrace upon terrace, from the palace of the Maccabees to the summit where Herod's palace overlooked the city. It was only a brief glimpse, for as the festal party continued, the city was again hidden from view.

This crowd had a life of its own. They celebrated the supposed coming of their King with words reported by Mark. However, fickle would be their devotion to One they thought would rule them, for soon they would all shout "Crucify Him" with all the anger that only a mob could stimulate. Their celebration as they walked with the Lord towards Jerusalem, though heartfelt, was superficial. "Hosanna! Blessed is He who comes in the name of the Lord! Blessed is the kingdom of our father David that comes in the name of the Lord! Hosanna in the highest!" (Mark 11:9, 10).

But for our Lord, there was no such joy. He knew He had not come to rule. He knew that His kingdom on earth had to wait until so many more prophecies would be fulfilled. Jerusalem was not to be the place of His immediate rule. Instead, there would be suffering when all the dreams of the crowds and even of His own disciples would be torn down and discarded into the trash can of history.

The whole group continued around the Mount of Olives, the path mounting until it reached a platform of rock near the summit. There their view was filled with the whole city rising out of the depths of the Kidron Valley. They paused, and Luke records that Jesus wept over the city when the city came into view (see Luke 19:41).

The Greek words Luke used express the depths of emotions felt in the Lord's Spirit at that time. This was not like the Lord's weeping over the grave of Lazarus. This was a loud and deep lamentation, His heart almost breaking over the city He loved. The deep feelings of our Lord for His own city are aptly expressed in His words to the scribes and Pharisees.

"O Jerusalem, Jerusalem, the one who kills the prophets and stones those who are sent to her! How often I wanted to gather your children together, as a hen gathers her chicks under her wings, but you were not willing!" (Matt. 23:37).

They descended into the Kidron Valley and then completed the brief climb into the city through the golden gate. The Lord then turned about, left the crowds, and returned to Bethany with His disciples. Tomorrow was Monday, and it had its own burden of activity in the city. Now there were only five days left until His final walk to the cross.

In His Footsteps

It was a fickle crowd I joined that day. Fickle and utterly superficial in its words and emotions, which, in spite of their superficiality, harbored the truth of the One who was riding the foal of an ass. I find no suggestion in the record that He was attentive to their words or actions. Instead, His inner eyes were focused on the city beyond the Kidron Valley, the city that He loved. He wept for those grey stones and all those who had profaned His name.

His outpouring of heartbreaking grief astonished me. I could have accepted His righteous judgment and His condemnation of those who had killed the prophets. I could have believed in His anger at the many who had thrown their sons into the fires of Moloch below the walls of the city and who had defiled His name with the worship of foreign gods. But grief? All my natural inclinations rebelled at the idea.

As part of that noisy crowd, I had to assess my own motives in following Him and the depth of my own search to know the One who would die to save the world. Would He pass over my superficiality with the disdain it deserved? Or would He weep over me who had offended Him in so many ways? The answers to my questions lay in an event that was still five days away. Until that terrible event unfolded, I had to continue my walk in His footsteps to Golgotha.

Chapter Four
MONDAY: You Have Made It a Den of Thieves

The Fig Tree Had No Fruit

Sunday of that last week was a day of deep and harrowing grief, as He wept over the city that bore His name, where He would die, and from which He would one day rule. That Sunday He fulfilled the word of the prophet Isaiah: "A Man of sorrows and acquainted with grief" (Isa. 53:3). He then retired to the restful environment of the home in Bethany.

After the night's rest, He left Bethany for the walk to Jerusalem. It was Monday, according to our reckoning, and that day another side of our Lord's character was revealed. It was to be a day of judgment, fulfilling what He Himself told His disciples that the Father had committed all judgment to the Son (see John 5:22).

As He and His disciples took the road from Bethany around the Mount of Olives to Jerusalem, they passed a fig tree growing on a little rise not far from the path (see Mark 11:13). To the casual passerby it was only a fig tree, but the spread of green hid an unfortunate truth. The fig tree carried no fruit, but it was a well-known fact that even in spring, the last of the winter figs could sometimes be found hidden among the new spring foliage.

It was early morning and Mark reports that Jesus was hungry. He must have told them, for how else would they have known? And perhaps His hunger signified something else. He went to the fig tree, and finding no fruit, He cursed the fig tree. Matthew tells us that the fig tree withered immediately, but Mark reports that they found the fig tree withered the next morning when they passed that way (see Matt. 21:18; Mark 11:20, 21).

The accounts of Matthew and Mark cause us to wonder why Jesus cursed the fig tree. Being the Son of God, He would have known exactly what the state of that tree was and that it bore no fruit. Was He grieved because He was hungry and had nothing to eat? Highly unlikely. Perhaps it was to teach His disciples and us across the centuries a lesson of some kind? And if so, what was the lesson? And were the images of the fig tree and the Lord's hunger images pointing us to other truths? I believe so.

In the Old Testament writings, as the Lord knew well, the fig tree was often associated with God's judgment of the land and its people. But in the Lord's own words recorded in the New Testament, we find further references to fig trees, and we can make a credible assumption that this fig tree was a symbol of Israel, both its land and its people.

In Jerusalem, the Lord had told a parable of judgment about a fig tree, and we can venture an interpretation though none is given in the Scriptures. "A certain man had a fig tree planted in his vineyard, and he came seeking fruit on it and found none. Then he said to the keeper of his vineyard, 'Look, for three years I have come seeking fruit on this fig tree and find none. Cut it down; why does it use up the ground?'" (Luke 13:6, 7).

The vineyard represents the whole earthly realm of our Lord God. The One who planted the fig tree is our God. The fig tree is one of the symbols of Israel, and the Keeper of the vineyard is our Lord Himself, the Christ and Messiah. The three years that the Owner of the vineyard came seeking fruit from the fig tree could refer to the ministry of the Lord Jesus among His people for He told His disciples that He had not been sent to anyone other than the lost sheep of the house of Israel (see Matt. 15:24).

In this parable I believe that the fruit He looked for among His own people was what Paul called the fruit of righteousness (see Phil. 1:11). In Jesus' day there was religion in abundance. The Pharisees and scribes were famous for their religious activities and for their decrees about temple observances and tithes and sacrifices. They fulfilled the letter of the law, but neglected the weightier matters that underpinned the law's observance (see Matt. 23:23). In fact, the leaders of His people confused religion with godliness. By forsaking inner godliness, they had taught themselves to be content with the outer forms of religion practiced by men and women around the world

David knew the difference between religion and godliness when he wrote Psalm 51. He wrote these words right after Nathan the prophet had confronted him, and this psalm reflects the true heart of our God and of His Son when He passed by that fig tree.

"For you do not desire sacrifice, or else I would give it; You do not delight in burnt offering. The sacrifices of God are a broken spirit, a broken and contrite heart—these, O God, You will not despise" (Ps. 51:16, 17).

Our Lord's hunger was not for the fruit that religion produces, represented by the missing fruit on the fig tree. He desired the true fruit of righteousness, the fruit that is the evidence of godliness. The Lord's stomach was not empty; His hunger was for the fruit His own people should have been producing.

With the teachings and practices of the scribes and Pharisees, the Lord found religious works in abundance, but the faith needed for His people to please the Father was largely absent (see Heb. 11:6). Certainly the various fruits of the Spirit described by Paul in his letter to the Galatian churches were not widely experienced among the Jewish leaders and their people, though there were exceptions, notably Nicodemus, Joseph of Arimathea, and the poor widow woman He would later encounter in the temple grounds.

In the parable of the fig tree, the Lord pronounced judgment (see Luke 13:6, 7). Likewise, He pronounced judgment on Jerusalem when He told His disciples that not one stone of the temple would be left standing on another (see Matt. 24:2). Around forty years later, the judgment was fulfilled when Roman legions under the command of Titus sacked the city and the fig tree that was indeed producing no fruit was dug up and cast aside.

In the account of the fig tree on the Mount of Olives, the Lord's judgment for the city and His people had begun. But His judgment did not end there. He would soon enter the temple grounds and there His judgment would again be expressed.

Temple Markets

Jesus and His disciples left the fig tree and passed around the slope of the Mount of Olives to the place where the road from Bethany met the road from Jericho. There they could see the walls of the city Jesus loved rising above the Kidron Valley. Prominently displayed above the city walls was Herod's temple, the renovated successor to Solomon's temple. They descended into the Kidron Valley and then ascended to the golden gate. Once they passed through, they had entered the temple grounds.

There are no records of what was on the Lord's heart when He saw the market stalls and the money changers' tables. Was it grief at the desecration of that holy place? Was He overwhelmed with anger at what His own people had done in the place God had sanctified so long ago?

He would have known how Solomon had brought the ark of the covenant and placed it in the inner sanctuary. During that time the glory of God filled the temple. When Jesus entered the temple grounds, the glory had long departed. And once the physical embodiment of that glory entered into their presence, their eyes could not see Him or understand who it was that stood among them. Instead of God's peace and glory, there was now the unholy bustle of buying and selling as well as the clutter of the market place.

When the temple was dedicated to the service and worship of the Lord God, it was filled with the sounds of prayer and revelation. Now, it was filled with the clamor of people bargaining over the price of a lamb or two pigeons or the correct amount to be paid in temple tax. They were even arguing over the exchange rate for the people seeking to change Roman or Greek or Egyptian or Persian or Syrian money into the temple money the rulers had decided was necessary for transactions in the temple grounds.

When Jesus entered the temple, He would have heard the market clamor of people while they were buying, selling, and yelling at each other across the money changers' tables, with the whole area filled with the bleating of sheep and the noises of animals for sale.

When Solomon dedicated the temple, the Lord described His part in that dedication.

"I have consecrated this house which you have built to put My name there [in the temple] forever, and My eyes and My heart will be there perpetually" (1 Kings 9:3).

So much had changed. So much had been forsaken. Those in authority had trampled underfoot the blessings the Lord God had given to His temple for profit. And no one profited more than the high priest and his family.

The Lord had created the position of the high priest, and Aaron, Moses' brother, was the first He sanctified for that service. When Aaron was dressed in the high priestly robes, a turban was placed on his head. A gold plaque was placed on the turban, which said, "HOLINESS TO THE LORD" (Exod. 39:30). The words show that the high priest is set apart for the Lord, to hear His words, to stand between the people and their God, and to present a sacrifice once a year in the Most Holy Place for the forgiveness of the peoples' sins. This was the commandment brought down through the centuries. But how far had the glory of that tradition departed from the temple and from the high priest's family?

Ancient writings tell us of a curse an eminent rabbi pronounced on the high priest's family. It is said that they were great hoarders of money, that they were very rich, and that they used violence to despoil the common priests of their due revenues. And profit taking was kept in the family. Another of the Hebrew documents tells us that some of the high priest's sons were also high priests, but other sons were treasurers, and their sons were assistant treasurers. These treasurers used their servants to intimidate those who would not pay.

There are also details in these documents of luxurious living, gluttony, wastefulness, and of general dissoluteness. It is no wonder that our Lord pronounced this judgment on what He saw when He told the crowd in the temple precincts that the temple was a house of prayer, which they had made into a den of thieves (see Matt. 21:13).

The Praise of the Children

There is a wonderful light side to the gravity of this account. There was rejoicing that day in the temple, for the Son of God had truly come into His own house. He was finally about to fulfill one of the purposes of His anointing: to heal the blind. Matthew reports, "The blind and the lame came to Him in the temple, and He healed them" (Matt. 21:14; see also Luke 4:18). The children who were present that day saw the lame and blind healed and looked upon the face of the One who had healed the suffering, and they cried out, "Hosanna to the Son of David!" (Matt. 21:15). The children acknowledged Him while the rulers of His own people did not.

So the first day of judgment came to an end. On the following day, He and His disciples would return to the temple where His judgment of all those who had desecrated that holy place and forsaken their relationship with the Most Holy One would continue. And perhaps with the praise of the children ringing in His ears, He left the temple and returned to Bethany.

In His Footsteps

Who could blame them? These religious rulers were only doing what was so common in the world of men: making a profit by whatever means and indulging their desires for good food, wealth, and rich possessions. But there was a hidden side to their indulgences. Perhaps without knowing it they had turned the ways of the kingdom of God into a kingdom of the world, and in doing so, they had let all the practices of that other world intrude into and corrupt the kingdom of our God.

I was born into that human world, and as I stood by in the temple, I acknowledged that I knew many of its ways. And while I could understand the indulgences and desires of the chief priests and those who followed in their benighted footsteps, I also had to acknowledge that Someone greater had come into the temple, and His ways had precedence.

It would have been so easy to excuse myself and the ways of the world that still clung to me like dirty substantial cobwebs while standing in the temple that day, but I could not. The temple in which He stood had been made to be a place of prayer devoted to submission to the Prince of righteousness.

In the same way, this physical house in which I dwell, the human body that has grown up around me and which I fill all too well, was designed for another purpose. It was not meant to be the home for desire, wealth, or the recipient of good food and wine, which is completely against the ways of the world into which I was born. I understood that day that the chief priests and their families had prostituted the purposes God had for His own house. Unlike the worldly ways of desire and self-indulgence, only prayer and worship would glorify God.

Paul told the disciples at the church in Corinth that my body, like the temple, was not my own. I learned from Paul that my body was not my own, for by His death on the cross He had purchased it for His own purposes. My responsibility was to use my body to glorify my Lord (see 1 Cor. 6:20). And that was the challenge I faced that day in the temple. It was as though His eyes caught mine over the money changers' tables, and He imposed on me the challenge that would take me the final steps to Golgotha where the redemption of my soul would be complete.

Chapter Five
TUESDAY: You Shall Love the Lord Your God

Introduction

The last Tuesday of the Lord's human life was a very crowded day involving teachings, parables, denunciations of the Jewish leaders delivered in the temple precincts, and prophecies relating to the end of times delivered to His disciples on the Mount of Olives. I have divided discussion of these events into three separate chapters.

In this document the term "temple" includes its porches, grounds, and precincts but not the interior of the temple. The sequence of chapter headings is also arbitrary, for there is no way of knowing the chronological sequence of the events of that day.

Two days before Passover, Jesus came to the temple with His disciples. In that place and for the last time, He spoke with five groups of people. Four groups were antagonistic with one person honestly wanting to see Jesus. And in the temple precincts, like a counterpoint to the devious opposition, Jesus observed one solitary widow bringing her gift to the Father. After these things took place, a number of Greek proselytes came to Him to gain a further understanding of who He really was.

His disciples were also with Him, so we have four accounts of what happened that day. The reason why they believe He addressed both teachings and parables was perhaps to equip them for the difficult days that were soon to overwhelm them. In this chapter we will examine His encounters with these people in the temple precincts. The following chapter will be devoted to two parables and eight woes He pronounced, also within the temple grounds, against the elders and chief priests.

But that day did not end when His work in the temple area was complete. The third chapter will also be devoted to that significant Tuesday when, after He left the city with His disciples, He crossed the Kidron Valley and found a convenient place on the slope of the Mount of Olives. It was there that He spoke about the end of days and left them with His final parables.

There was One other in the temple precincts that day. John left us with so many intimate details of the Lord's last hours, and he also recorded the intimate jewel of a conversation between the Lord soon to die and His own Father. We do not see Him, but we hear the Father's recognition of what His Son would achieve for the world through terrible pain and unspeakable suffering.

It seems that there is a hidden pattern behind the four accounts of Jesus' encounters with people in the temple grounds. Each of the groups that opposed Him during His ministry was present that day and engaged in the most devious kinds of dialogue. These four groups represent the whole of the people of Israel in their roles as rulers, teachers, lawyers, and political opportunists.

The image of the barren fig tree is justly represented in these four groups, though the common people are not included, except in the figure of one solitary woman. She was also a Hebrew bound up in the edicts of her religion, but with an honest heart bringing her gift to the One she worshipped.

The world of the Gentiles is represented in the persons of the Greek proselytes, who make up a fifth group. Gentiles who had become Jews wanted to see Jesus, and so, together with the sixth group of His disciples, the scene in the temple grounds was complete.

Chief Priests, Scribes, and Elders

They appear almost as a single group, but there were considerable differences between the three groups Jesus encountered that day. Chief priests included those who had formerly been chief priests and were responsible for the administration of religious services associated with the temple and the synagogue. The scribes were teachers and specialists in all legal matters relating to the oral and written laws. The elders, on the other hand, were members of the Sanhedrin, the Supreme Court responsible for all things Jewish. Elders could have been Pharisees or Sadducees, and members of both groups could also be members of the Sanhedrin.

The fact that they came to Jesus that day suggests that there had been a meeting of the Sanhedrin discussing what to do about this troublesome Nazarene, who stood opposed to all that they stood for. They were not yet able to arrest Him, for they did not have sufficient evidence to ensure a conviction. They came that day to the temple seeking to trap Him and give them just cause for His crucifixion.

They came to Jesus after reports reached them of His assault on the money changers and on those who bought and sold for profit in the temple. They had seen Him teaching the crowds and witnessed the miracles of healing in the temple grounds. Their anger against the Lord was mounting, so they challenged Him with a question about the source of the authority He used to heal and perform miracles on the temple grounds (see Mark 11:28).

Members of the Sanhedrin had a problem with authority. In their tradition a teacher could only teach if he had been granted the authority to do so by the Supreme Court. In this way their religious system fed on itself. They knew that He could not teach under their authority. And they could never acknowledge that Jesus' authority came from God, for that would seriously undermine their own position and lay them open to opposition from the lower orders of their society, who had been taught that the authority of the Sanhedrin had come from God. And their reasoning left them with only one conclusion: Jesus' authority came from the prince of demons, Beelzebub. So in the hopes of trapping Him, they asked where He obtained His authority.

In His reply the Lord directed them to the one person who epitomized their problem: John the Baptist. People acknowledged John as a prophet sent from God. The Lord answered their question by challenging them with a question about the source of the baptism of John the Baptist, whether it was from heaven or from men (see Mark 11:30).

They were caught on the horns of a dilemma. If they answered that John's baptism was from God then they opened themselves to the obvious counter, 'Why did you not believe him?' If they answered that John's baptism was from men then they invited the opposition of the crowds, who acknowledged that John was a prophet sent from God. They kept silent so that their words would not incriminate them.

In return, the chief priests, scribes, and elders got their answer when He told them He also would not reveal the source of His authority (see Mark 11:33).

Pharisees and Herodians

Mark reports that they, probably the Sanhedrin, sent the Pharisees and Herodians to catch the Lord in His words. Every Pharisee belonged to a religious community of laymen, most often merchants and tradesmen. Their concern was with the purity of the law, the Torah written down by Moses, and with the oral law, which they held to be just as inspired and authoritative as the written law.

On the other hand, the Herodians were a political group who supported the power of the dynasty of Herod the Great, notably Herod Antipas, who ruled as a Roman appointee in the province of Galilee. The Herodians were committed to the status quo and were antagonistic to the teaching and miracles of our Lord and became particularly aggressive when He taught about the coming kingdom of God. All these things upset the status quo to which these two groups were committed. Attacks on the Lord from established religion were mounting.

The trap was set with their question about the legality of paying taxes to Caesar (see Mark 12:14). If the Lord said that it was not lawful to pay Caesar's taxes, He would be taking a position tantamount to opposition to the governing power. If He said that it was lawful, He would have incurred the anger of the local populace, who objected to the payment of any tax to the hated occupying power. The Lord's response was precise and to the point when He told them that they had two debts they had to honor—one to Caesar and the other to God (see Mark 12:17).

In our Lord's words, we have the strongest statement of His acknowledgment that the governing power had been set in place by the Father, as well as His acceptance that submission to the governing power would send Him to crucifixion. In submitting to Pilate's decision to crucify Him, He would indeed be rendering to Caesar the things that were Caesar's. Jesus saw that behind Caesar's decision was the decision of the One who was sending Him on that shameful path to a lonely death, when all, including His own Father, would desert Him.

The Sadducees

They came to Jesus with a question. It was not a serious question asked by someone seeking to know the truth. Rather, it was like the Pharisees and Herodians before them attempting to "entangle Him in His talk" (Matt. 22:15). Their question was so hypothetical that it was almost meaningless. If a woman married a man and he died, she would marry again. And if this were to happen seven times, whose wife would she be in the resurrection?

Their question was in fact a denial of their own teachings for they held that when a person had breathed his last, the soul itself also died. They also believed that there was no resurrection. All the things the Sadducees believed ran counter to the truth that would be soon unveiled. Jesus' death would be followed by His resurrection, giving the lie to this part of the Sadducees' teaching. And through His death and resurrection, the prince of demons and of the kingdom of darkness would also be defeated.

Jesus' reply exposed their ignorance. He told them that they neither knew the Scriptures nor the power of God (see Matt. 22:29), and then added fuel to the fire by referring them to the words of Scriptures where God Himself had said, "God is not the God of the dead, but of the living" (Matt. 22:32). His death and resurrection was to demonstrate the power of God over death and over the prince of darkness.

The Lawyer

Matthew and Mark record the fourth question one of the Jewish leaders brought to Jesus that day. But there was a significant difference between the previous questions and the question this man brought forward. The first three questions were theoretical and brought by groups who solely wanted to establish grounds for His indictment and death. The fourth question was brought by an individual lawyer, and although Matthew tells us that it was originally meant to be a trick, his question was still about a subject that was central to his belief system; it was about the law he revered. Mark's words suggest that the lawyer had come to a change of heart while listening to Jesus and had, perhaps secretly, admired Jesus' previous responses. Because of that admiration, he was able to find the courage to ask a question about an issue he found compelling and that had the potential to profoundly affect His relationship with the Almighty.

Without knowing it the lawyer had come before a door leading into the life and affairs of the kingdom of heaven. Jesus' response would not only give him the key to the door but the means by which he could pass through into the life of heaven itself. The Lord's answer was to remind them that their first obligation was to love the Lord their God with all their heart, soul, mind, and strength (see Mark 12:30).

I can imagine that for that brief yet eternal moment all the inhabitants in heaven stood still. The love that Jesus spoke about was central to their beings, as it is the essence of the nature of God Himself. It was the epitome of all their actions in obeying the will of the Father. It was the essence of the purpose God spoke about in the Garden: humanity was made in the image of God, in the image of love Himself, and they should reproduce, populate, rule, and make it a place where love was fully established. In this way the earth would be filled with God's love, true love, divine love, *agape* love.

What the Lord didn't tell the lawyer was that this kind of love was never one way. It was always intended to be returned. As the aged apostle John put it, "We love Him because He first loved us" (1 John 4:19). This truth could have changed the life of the lawyer forever had he asked that question after Pentecost when the love of God was poured into the hearts of those who had given their lives to Him. But for the lawyer, as for so many in Jerusalem, *agape* love was unknown; however, all that would change in the next few days.

The Poor Widow

Inserted into the story of that Tuesday in the temple is a very short record of the actions of a poor widow. It is as though it has been set in counterpoint to the events that preceded it. Probably seated on one of the steps of the temple, our Lord could see the containers into which the devout and the religious could leave their offerings. Each container, shaped like an inverted trumpet, bore inscriptions about whether the gift was to make up for past neglect, to pay for specified sacrifices, or to provide incense, wood, or for other gifts.

Some offerings, like those brought by the Pharisees, were dropped into the container with much ostentation. The gift giver would create attention to the size of the amount and the amount of time it would take the coins to rattle their way to the bottom all in hopes that they would be observed and applauded for their supposed generosity. This was not the case for the poor widow.

Jesus watched as she brought her two small coins, the minimum amount that could legally be given, and dropped them into the vessel. We infer that she hoped that no one had noticed her, but of course the Lord had, knowing not only the exact amount of her offering but the state of her heart. Mark reports, "He called His disciples to Himself and said to them, 'Assuredly, I say to you that this poor widow has put in more than all those who have given to the treasury; for they all put in out of their abundance, but she out of her poverty put in all that she had, her whole livelihood'" (Mark 12:43, 44).

The Greek Proselytes

Sometime during that day, a group of Greek proselytes came to Philip and asked if they could be given permission to meet with Jesus. The King James Version words it as such: "We would see Jesus" (John 12:21). In English, the word "see" refers to the physical act of seeing something or someone. In Greek, the word carries a fuller meaning, referring not only the act of seeing but also the desire for a perception of the Lord who was nearby, to understand something of who He is. Philip told Andrew and together they went to Jesus and told Him of the Greeks' request.

Undoubtedly, Jesus understood what the Greeks desired, and His words helped them see far beyond the appearance of the Person in front of them. For the first time that day, He revealed Himself to His listeners.

"The hour has come that the Son of Man should be glorified. Most assuredly, I say to you, unless a grain of wheat falls into the ground and dies, it remains alone; but if it dies, it produces much grain" (John 12:23, 24).

And then putting into words the purpose that had guided Him throughout His life, He explained in words that only spanned a few minutes but had enough power to apply to all His disciples throughout all ages. He expounded on the spiritual burden His disciples have to carry within themselves forever. "He who loves his life will lose it, and he who hates his life in this world will keep it for eternal life. If anyone serves Me, let him follow Me; and where I am, there My servant will be also. If anyone serves Me, him My Father will honor" (John 12:25, 26).

The Witness of the Father

There was another, though unseen, Person in the temple grounds that day. He was listening when the Lord turned His eyes heavenward to tell the Father that His soul was troubled, but He quickly affirmed that the Father's purpose was for Him to come to the trial He was about to face (see John 12:27, 28).

When the Father heard the words of His Son, He broke His silence and told Him that He had already glorified His name through the acts and teachings of His Son, and He would glorify it again through His death and resurrection.

What wonder there is in the Father's words! He was not speaking only of Jesus but of His own purposes since the world began. For the Father is the One who intended that His name and His love should fill the earth (see Gen. 1:26). That glory was lost at Eden. Now, it would be restored through the lives of those who would follow the Son (see Rom. 8:29).

There is a postscript to Jesus' words and to the words of the Father. "Now is the judgment of this world; now the ruler of this world will be cast out. And I, if I am lifted up from the earth, will draw all peoples to Myself" (John 12:31, 32).

After a final comment from the crowd, Jesus ended His words in the temple by telling them of the light and also of the darkness that would soon overtake Him. He is the Light of the world, and they were to walk in the light while He was with them. Then He brought their attention back to the relationship with Himself and concluded His words in the temple precincts with the instruction to His disciples that while He was with them they had the obligation to believe in the Light so that they might become sons of Light (see John 12:36).

In His Footsteps

As I heard all these things that day in the temple, I had to ask myself, "Where do I belong?" Which of these diverse groups of people the Lord spoke with that day truly epitomized my own being? The first three groups I readily stepped away from. My faith was inward not outward in religious observances like theirs, and I had no combative questions designed to trip Him up. But then I was faced with my Lord's conversation with the lawyer.

This Jew asked the question I should have asked. "Which is the first commandment of all?" (Mark 12:28). And as I listened to their discussion, I had to admit that this question carried with it the burden of my own soul. At that time I reminded myself of the meanings of two Greek words. The first is the word the Lord used that is translated to "love" in the English language, and that is *agape*. The second is the word the lawyer used, which is translated as "first" and that is *protos*.

I had learned that *agape* refers to the love that springs from admiration, respect, and veneration of the one being loved because of the choice to love rather than because of an impulse. It also puts service for the other ahead of the benefits for oneself, and it does not permit the costs of service to get in the way of that service.

The word the lawyer used in referring to the first commandment is *protos*, which refers to the place I must give the commandment to love the Lord my God. Love for Him must be first in the use of my time, first in the order of my priorities, first in my use of the spaces I inhabit, and first in the order of dignity I give to all the elements of my faith.

I also had to admit that day in the temple that I had to love Him with all my heart, soul, mind, and strength. It had to be a consistent love and not just randomly here and there. I could not just pull it out when it pleased me and put it away when it did not. Nor was that love to be expressed only when others gathered for worship. It had to hold true when I was alone and when I was burdened with the pains of this world. I had to love God in my frustrations and distractions that followed me into and through relationships that had gone awry. It had to be the part of me that responded when my old nature out of Eden persisted with its stubborn desires and threatened to overwhelm love itself. Then I had to take my stand and give back to Him what He had come to earth to give to me.

I understood the first commandment when it applied to my love for Him, but when I turned the equation around I ran into an enormous difficulty. He is the essence of love and loving Him does not find an obstacle in His nature and being. But when I figured out that *agape* also refers to Him loving me, my human reasoning ran into a brick wall. He is immensely loveable, if one could use that word without blasphemy. However, I am not. So how could He admire and reverence me even though I am one of those He created in His own image? And why does He put Himself out to serve me when I am the most ignoble and unreceptive of beings? At that time, three days before Golgotha loomed its ugly head over history, I did not have an answer to my ponderings and perhaps I never will.

I also believed, as I had been taught, that loving another is costly. Counting the cost of loving Him is not a particularly daunting challenge, but then I turned the issue around and looked at it from the Father's point of view. What would be the cost to the Father and to His beloved Son if they loved me in that ultimate manner? I had to know, not what doctrines taught me, but what would be displayed on the cross three days from now.

Chapter Six
TUESDAY: Whitewashed Tombs

Introduction

The temple narratives include a number of parables relating to the kingdom and to the Lord's condemnation of the Pharisees. For the sake of convenience, the parables that deal with the Pharisees have been included in this chapter. Parables that deal with the kingdom of heaven will be discussed in a later chapter.

Blind Leaders of the Blind

There were only three days left until our Lord's crucifixion; three days full of grief and indignation as well as our Lord's quiet love for those who had surrendered their lives to Him. He also had only three days in which to prepare His disciples for the trials that lay ahead. It was three days in which the purposes of the Father would be fulfilled, and three days in which His divine nature could be fully expressed among those He would encounter on the way to the cross.

He came to the temple and encountered the different groups of people we examined in the previous chapter. We now have to consider the part of His nature that was deeply grieved and indignant because of these people, which causes us to also look closely at His judgment of them, as they had the responsibility of being shepherds to His own people. We come to His condemnation of the blind leading the blind, which took its form in two parables and eight woes.

John the Baptist called the leaders of the Jews a brood of vipers (see Luke 3:7). Jesus called them whitewashed tombs when he encountered them that day in the temple (see Matt. 23:27). He understood everything about them: their words, their traditions, their addiction to public display, their pretensions to public piety, their adherence to doctrinal truth at the expense of godliness, and their overwhelming distrust, hate, and fear of our Lord. Jesus knew it all.

It was probably in the afternoon of that Tuesday when Jesus spoke to the crowd and to His disciples about the blind leaders of the blind and denounced them as always being prepared to place heavy burdens on men's shoulders (see Matt. 23:4). He described them as delighting in putting on an outward show with broad phylacteries and enlarged borders on their garments all the while loving the best seats in the synagogues (see Matt. 23:2–7).

It is tempting to stand with the Lord and agree with the terrible denunciations He brought against these men. But if we look only at Jesus' words, we may be limited to the externals. We need a model that will help us understand who these men were in their inner beings, but the same model must also help us understand such men as Nicodemus and Joseph of Arimathea who were both Pharisees, as well as one of the most prolific biblical writers, Paul, who was also a Pharisee. And last of all, the same model will help us understand ourselves.

Religion and Godliness

The model we need to understand the inner dealings of all who profess His name is woven around two Greek words. The first is *threskeia*, which can be translated "religion" and refers to the outward ceremonial observance of religion, religion's external forms, which are normally performed by man's old, unredeemed nature, the flesh (see Gal. 5:19–21).

This Greek word is opposed to our second Greek word, *eusebeia*, which is usually translated "godliness" and refers to our real, true, vital, inner relationship in the Spirit with God our Father; His eternal Spirit united with our redeemed and reborn spirit (see John 3:3, 5; Ezek. 11:19; Rom. 7:6).

The practice of religion largely depends on human energy. The experience of godliness, on the other hand, cannot make use of human energies. It is always an experience of the spirit, His Spirit united with our spirit. Godliness requires the combination of the energies of our reborn spirits with the energies of the Spirit of the Father. It is as Paul wrote to the church at Philippi, "Work out your own salvation with fear and trembling; for it is God who works in you both to will and to do for His good pleasure" (Phil. 2:12, 13). This cooperative relationship between the disciple and the One who redeemed us is the essence of godliness.

Now we can make some observations about the scribes and Pharisees, just as Jesus did that Tuesday in Jerusalem. The word that fits them is *threskeia*, religion in all its outward forms, which was denounced by the Lord in His parables and His eight woes. But when we come to Nicodemus and Joseph of Arimathea, who were both Pharisees, we come to a puzzle, for it is certain that both of them practiced their religion. We have to conclude that within these two men there was true godliness and that they chose to express their godliness through the outward acts of their religion.

The practice of religion on its own in today's world excludes godliness, but true godliness does not exclude a follower's choice to express his or her godliness through a range of religious activities.

Paul began with religion, but on the Damascus Road, he entered the real, true, vital relationship with his Lord, which is the essence of godliness. He then turned his back on the religion of his fathers in favor of godliness. Because there was no godliness in the men Jesus faced that day in the temple, they fell under the condemnation that He expressed in two parables and eight woes.

The Two Sons

In His first parable, Jesus told of a man who had two sons and a vineyard. He told the first son to go and work in the vineyard. At first, the son refused and then a little later agreed to go. The owner of the vineyard then told the second son to go, and he agreed but later refused.

Jesus then asked the chief priests and elders which of the two sons did the will of the father. The answer was obvious. The first son had done so. Jesus then pointed them to the meaning of the parable. The vineyard represented the people of Israel. The first son represented the tax collectors and prostitutes who, when invited to enter the kingdom, had refused. At first, they persisted in their reprobate lifestyle of debauchery and criminal extortion, but Matthew records that afterwards these men and women regretted their decision. The term Jesus used of the first son was *metamelomai*, which means to be dissatisfied with oneself, to regret one's decision, or to register anxiety because of a past decision.

The lifestyle and sins of the prostitutes and sinners had shut them out of God's promises for those who belonged in His vineyard, the children of Israel. But their repentance had faced them in the opposite direction and as Jesus affirmed, the sinners and tax collectors would go into the kingdom of God before they would (see Matt. 21:31).

The chief priests and elders, on the other hand, were represented by the second son, who said he would go and labor in God's vineyard but then refused. Jesus, with very sharp and deliberately pointed and hard-hitting words, told them, "For John came to you in the way of righteousness, and you did not believe him; but tax collectors and harlots believed him; and when you saw it, you did not afterward relent and believe him" (Matt. 21:32).

The difference between the two sons was couched in repentance. The chief priests and elders were steeped in their religious traditions, and they believed that they were on the right path. Repentance was more than unnecessary; it was out of the question. They completely lacked the capacity for repentance of a past direction, and thus lost the will to alter that direction.

Immediately, the Lord told these same people another parable that deepened His condemnation of their religion and undoubtedly confirmed them in their commitment to have Him put to death.

The Wicked Vinedressers

In this parable the Lord spoke of the landowner sending his servants to receive his share of the produce of his vineyard. They beat one, killed one, and stoned another. Then the landowner sent other servants, and they were treated in the same way. Finally, he sent his son, and he was cast out of the vineyard and then killed.

His hearers knew what the parable meant. They had the witness of Isaiah who stated that the house of Israel was the Lord's vineyard (see Isa. 5:7). By inference, those who had charge of the vineyard under the hand of the Lord God were those who belligerently stood around the Lord that day in the temple.

In this parable Jesus spoke about the servants God had sent into the vineyard to receive His share of the fruit. He was referring to the prophets the Father had sent. In the temple that afternoon, our Lord spoke of Zechariah, the son of Berechiah, whom the leaders had murdered between the temple and the altar (see Matt. 23:35).

The name Zechariah was familiar to those to whom the parable was addressed. But there are only two who fulfill the Lord's description: the prophet Zechariah who wrote the second to last book in the Old Testament, but there is no record of his death. The other Zechariah was the son of Jehoiada, the high priest in the reign of Joash, the king of Judah. He was a godly man, and he spoke out against the apostasy of the people. However, he was stoned to death in the temple courts by orders of the king (see 2 Chron. 24:19–21).

After the first servants the Father sent to His vineyard were killed, the Father sent others to proclaim His truth that He ordained for His people. The faithless men in charge killed these passionate truth-tellers as quickly as they could. The owner of the vineyard then sent His only Son. This caused the leaders of men in God's vineyard to reason among themselves: "But when the vinedressers saw the son, they said among themselves, 'This is the heir. Come, let us kill him and seize his inheritance.' So they took him and cast him out of the vineyard and killed him" (Matt. 21:38, 39).

It is notable that those responsible for God's vineyard in the parable had a motive for their actions. They did not just hope to kill Him but they also wanted to seize His inheritance. The inheritance was the vineyard itself, as it was redeemed, cleansed from all sin, and set apart for His glory. In this parable the Lord was speaking to the leaders of His people responsible for that vineyard. They could not and would not acknowledge that Jesus of Nazareth was the Messiah and that He was the true ruler in His vineyard. They only lusted after that responsibility and had taken it for themselves.

It is one of the ironies of history that our Lord was speaking of His death with the very people who would see Him crucified. And they knew it (see Matt. 21:45, 46).

The Lord had denounced the chief priests and Pharisees in these two parables, but there was still more to be said. In the temple and under instructions from His Father, Jesus pronounced eight woes that are also recorded by Matthew.

Denunciations

In the midst of the Lord's denunciations of the scribes and the Pharisees, the Lord changed the subject and gave His attention to His disciples and also to us across the centuries. It is useful to place His challenge to them and to us in the context of organized religion, which demands a performance that can be seen and assessed. We are not to be called rabbi, for the Lord Christ is our Teacher. Nor are we to call anyone Father, for there is only one Father, and He sits on the throne of glory in the heavens.

Unlike the scribes and Pharisees who delighted in exalting themselves, we are to humble ourselves before the Lord and before others. Jesus then left us with the challenge He Himself faced and lived out in His life: "But he who is greatest among you shall be your servant. And whoever exalts himself will be humbled, and he who humbles himself will be exalted" (Matt. 23:11, 12).

The Lord then went on to speak of eight woes that would come on the scribes and Pharisees. In reading Jesus' denunciations of the scribes and Pharisees, it is a serious mistake to restrict them to the Jewish leaders of our Lord's day. There is a broader application, for there are men, and I dare say women, who are modern counterparts of the scribes and Pharisees in our Christian world. Or in other words, there are elements of the religious attitudes of the scribes and Pharisees that surface in all of us. Such attitudes come to us through our natural tendencies that are a result of the sinful nature we inherited from our first ancestors.

Our task is to make it one of our life's works to fully understand these elements that earn our Lord's disapproval. We need to work for the renewal of our hearts and minds so that we may stand tall when we are before the judgment seat of our Christ (see Rom. 12:2; 2 Cor. 5:10).

In Jesus' statements about the scribes and Pharisees, He used a term that is translated as "woe," which simply means "alas." However, the term carries with it undertones of grief and indignation. Here, the indignation is for those who claimed to lead Israel but had been trapped in the most subtle of the adversary's devices, and the Lord's grief was for the common people, who had been blindly following leaders who were themselves blind. All of His people carried burdens of religious belief and behavior that many could not bear within their hearts and minds.

The First Woe

"But woe to you, scribes and Pharisees, hypocrites! For you shut up the kingdom of heaven against men; for you neither go in yourselves, nor do you allow those who are entering to go in" (Matt. 23:13).

One of the distinctive marks of the religion of the scribes and Pharisees is the separation between those in places of leadership, and those who, in human terms, are of a lower rank. This separation enabled those leaders to impose their own doctrinal standards or religious rules and practices on those they considered below them.

They had the power and authority to "shut up the kingdom of heaven against men." The common people in Israel—and in our day as well because this separation still exists—did not have such power, but in obediently following the doctrines of their leaders had become blind being led by the blind, acquiescent, unthinking, and believing without question

The separation between those who lead and those being led in the Christian church did not make its appearance in the apostolic church of the first century, where there was the stress of all being equal members of the one body. However, the second century was barely launched when this heresy (for it is a heresy) of the separation of the leaders and those being led made its appearance. Clement of Philippi writing around the end of the first and the beginning of the second centuries, and Tertullian of Carthage, writing a century later, made the distinction between clergy and laity and proceeded to ascribe power to the former. This distinction was epitomized by the Roman Catholic Church, which later taught that only those who had been confirmed by a priest could enter heaven.

There is an element of exclusive pride and religious arrogance in this characteristic of being a Pharisee. We have seen this aspect of religion many times throughout the history of the institutional church, and it is present in different guises and with different degrees of severity in many parts of the church today.

The teaching that only those who agree with a church's doctrine and practice can be admitted to active membership in a church is one aspect we have left of Phariseeism. Many leaders and church councils use these means to keep people in their church subservient and controlled, and they are also able to lock out those they consider undesirable, using their doctrine as a standard to keep people at bay. And those who do not measure up are not admitted.

The Second Woe

"Woe to you, scribes and Pharisees, hypocrites! For you devour widows' houses, and for a pretense make long prayers. Therefore you will receive greater condemnation" (Matt. 23:14).

The term "widow" includes all who are defenseless, vulnerable, and have no power or liberty to protest or to fight back. And to our discredit, there are people like this in every church who go unnoticed. For "devour," one can think of swallowing up something so that nothing remains or is visible. What was devoured, in this case, were widows' houses, which became absorbed into the property of those doing the devouring: the scribes and Pharisees.

It was not only material things such as goods and money that were devoured by the scribes and Pharisees. Many other non-material things also disappeared into the maw of their religion. These included such things as personal responsibility, accountability, and the right to make individual choices. The common people were also denied the right of access to the Father by the ones Jesus called hypocrites.

A second element in Jesus' denunciation of the scribes and Pharisees was another aspect of their outward show: "and for a pretense make long prayers." This aspect of their religion ran counter to the Lord's own teaching. Jesus taught that when His disciples prayed, they should not be like the hypocrites who loved to pray standing in the synagogues and on the street corners. Instead, the Lord taught them that the proper place for prayer was a secret place away from those who would applaud or decry their efforts. He taught them that God, who sees what happens in private, would reward them openly (see Matt. 6:5, 6).

The devouring of widows' houses and the denial of personal rights and responsibilities both have their counterpart in institutional Christianity. One of the great and enlightened teachings of the reformation is what has become known as "the priesthood of all believers" (see 1 Peter 2:9). It is a sad fact of institutional life that so many are content to remain passive and to leave the difficult problems to the clergy, claiming, "That is what they are paid for." One wonders if the modern counterparts of the scribes and Pharisees in contemporary Christianity would also receive the Lord's condemnation?

The Third Woe

"Woe to you, scribes and Pharisees, hypocrites! For you travel land and sea to win one proselyte, and when he is won, you make him twice as much a son of hell as yourselves" (Matt. 23:15).

A proselyte was someone who was a covert to Judaism. In other words, it was a Gentile who became a Jew. In the Jewish faith, there were strict procedures for becoming a proselyte. The applicant was first asked if he or she understood the abject position the Jews had in the eyes of the Gentile world. If the person understood and was willing to be associated with the Jews in the views of the world, the future proselyte went into a period of strict study. First, he or she had to master the easier aspects of the Jewish law and then go on to the more difficult aspects of the Torah. You could not simply know the Ten Commandments. You had to know the entire range of ceremonial and sacrificial laws. Once this was mastered, the person was baptized, given a new name, and told to leave behind all the elements of his or her past life including ties of kinship and marriage.

The first and third elements in the process would not have attracted the Lord's denunciation, but the second phase certainly did. This is what the Lord would have had in mind when He said, "You make him [the proselyte] twice as much a son of hell as yourselves."

The Lord knew that from the scribes' and Pharisees' point of view the law did not only involve what Moses had written down as dictated by the Spirit of the Lord, but it also included what the Jews called the oral law, which they held to have been given by God to Moses on Mount Sinai. They believed that the oral law had the same authority as the five books of Moses. In addition to the law itself, there were commentaries on the law that the scribes had made, and every proselyte had to be fully acquainted with these before he or she could be admitted as a Jew.

But one thing was left out in the formation of a proselyte: the heart of love that the Lord taught, which was the only way to truly fulfill all the requirements of the law (see Matt. 22:37–40). This is God's own love, *agape* love, poured out into our hearts by the Holy Spirit, and it is an expression of the heart and being of the Father.

Obtaining zeal was another part of becoming a true proselyte. The proselyte was able to gain zealousness for the law through some kind of transfer from his or her teacher. We are not exactly sure what the steps were in this process, but in essence, the proselyte was made in the image of his teacher. However, Jesus tells us that the outcome was worse than simply becoming like their misguided teacher. He tells us that a proselyte became twice as much a son of hell as his teacher. Paul, who was certainly not a proselyte, wrote about this transfer of zeal from his teacher Gamaliel to himself when he wrote to the church in Galatia and told them that he had advanced in the zealous practice of his faith and in the traditions of their fathers beyond his contemporaries (see Gal. 1:14 and Acts 22:3).

In this day and age, there are many who make disciples and say that they are fulfilling the Lord's command to go throughout the world and make disciples of all nations (see Matt. 28:19, 20). But there is a distinction between the Lord's intention and the intention that underlies so much evangelism today. Now, there are so many who are made followers of a particular church, a church leader, or a denomination, and this is contrary to the Lord's purpose that they be made disciples and followers of the Lord Himself.

The Fourth Woe

"Woe to you, blind guides, who say, 'Whoever swears by the temple, it is nothing; but whoever swears by the gold of the temple, he is obliged to perform it.' Fools and blind! For which is greater, the gold or the temple that sanctifies the gold? And, 'Whoever swears by the altar, it is nothing; but whoever swears by the gift that is on it, he is obliged to perform it'" (Matt. 23:16–18).

An oath is defined as a promise that is true and binding. An oath is something that the Lord God is called on to witness. One of the first recorded oaths was made during the last days of Abraham's life when he called his servant and told him to not allow Isaac to marry a Canaanite woman (see Gen. 24:3).

This was a binding promise, for the oath was made in the name of the Lord God. The Scriptures also refer to God swearing by His great name, by His holiness, and by His right hand and mighty arm (see Jer. 44:26; Amos 4:2; Isa. 62:8).

The scribes had a well-developed understanding of the patterns of oaths contained in the Scriptures. They did not only have understanding of the Scripture references, but they interpreted them in everyday situations. From these biblical patterns, they developed a wide range of things by which a Jew could swear an oath, and this was the background for the Lord's condemnation. One could swear by the temple, the gold of the temple, the altar, the gift on the altar, heaven, the throne of God, and by the One who sits on the throne.

Not content with these detailed prescriptions for swearing an oath, the scribes had to place them in some kind of order, so they decided which oath was greatest and which was least. And this was the focus of the Lord's condemnation. He wasn't focusing on the swearing of an oath, though he did have something to say about that (see Matt. 5:37). Rather, He was desperately trying to point out the scribes' practice of taking simple instruction, such a swearing an oath or relating to a Sabbath day's journey, and hedging it round with all sorts of limitations and conditions. I wonder how many books of doctrine and theology have been written that makes the simple truths of the gospel complicated.

The scribes and their colleagues justified this excessive list of applications and conditions as "putting a hedge around the law," for they taught that knowledge was equivalent to piety. The greater the knowledge one obtained, the greater the piety that was also obtained. They also believed that ordinary folk were not capable of great knowledge and were therefore held to be less pious than themselves.

This aspect of Pharisaism has its modern counterpart. Historically, the Catholic Church has believed that the ordinary folk were not able to interpret the Scriptures and this holy task had to be left to the priests, hence the lack of translations of the scriptures in local languages. Although that situation was remedied through such people as William Tyndale, who was strangled and burned at the stake, this aspect of Pharisaism still persists where church leaders attempt to put a hedge around the doctrines that establish their identities.

The Fifth Woe

"Woe to you, scribes and Pharisees, hypocrites! For you pay tithe of mint and anise and cummin, and have neglected the weightier matters of the law: justice and mercy and faith" (Matt. 23:23).

The scribes and Pharisees were particularly proud of two accomplishments: tithing and ritual purification. The Lord's fifth woe was directed against their practice of tithing while the sixth woe, as we will see, was directed against their focus on ritual purification. Unfortunately for them, these two practices were the central planks in the doctrinal structure they had erected around themselves.

The Jewish practice of tithing had a long and honorable history. The first injunctions are found in Leviticus where it is written, "And all the tithe [literally a tenth] of the land, whether of the seed of the land or of the fruit of the tree, is the Lord's. It is holy to the Lord" (Lev. 27:30). All that is clear and without debate, but the scribes prided themselves on their ability to interpret the law and define what "a tenth of the land" meant in practice.

References in Numbers, Deuteronomy, 2 Chronicles, and Nehemiah tell us that the tithe applied to grain, fruit, herds, flocks, wine, oil, and honey—there was no mention of tithing mint, cumin, or anise. These tithes stipulated in the Scriptures had to be brought into the storehouse of the temple so that they could be distributed to the Levites, who had not been granted land of their own from which they could derive a livelihood.

The scribes were not content with the simple pronouncements of the Scripture; they were obsessively intrigued by the minutiae of the law. They interpreted the term "land" to mean all that the land produced and could serve as food, which obviously included herbs. But their practice became absurd. According to their ruling, any householder growing one plant of cumin had to set aside a tenth of the leaves, stems, and seeds as a tithe to the Lord.

Focusing on the details at the expense of the greater themes of the law such as justice, mercy, and faith earned them the Lord's condemnation.

The Sixth Woe

"Woe to you, scribes and Pharisees, hypocrites! For you cleanse the outside of the cup and dish, but inside they are full of extortion and self-indulgence. Blind Pharisee, first cleanse the inside of the cup and dish, that the outside of them may be clean also" (Matt. 23:25, 26).

This is the second doctrinal plank of the Pharisee's religion: ritual purity. They insisted on making sure that the outside of a cup and dish was ritually clean and neglected its contents. The outside was symbolic of the observable practices of their religion such as using the appropriate prayers, bringing specified offerings, and being present for set rituals and ceremonies.

The scribes and Pharisees had no interest in the inner state of their own lives nor in the inner state of the lives of those they were supposed to lead. It was for that reason the Lord declared that they and their followers were full of extortion and self-indulgence. Matthew and Zacchaeus were the same, but their hearts changed once they met the Lord. The scribes and Pharisees refused to change, and their pride led to their downfall.

You and I can readily see the modern parallel of Jesus' statement of woe, where the observable performance of one's faith is of far greater importance than the inner state of the worshiper. It is tantamount to the spurious teaching that if one makes sure there is a satisfactory outward performance of religion, whether being present, giving one's offering, making a contribution to the life of the church, that the inner state of the believer will take care of itself. And for that the Lord's condemnation will surely apply.

The Seventh Woe

"Woe to you, scribes and Pharisees, hypocrites! For you are like whitewashed tombs which indeed appear beautiful outside, but inside are full of dead men's bones and all uncleanness. Even so you also outwardly appear righteous to men, but inside you are full of hypocrisy and lawlessness" (Matt. 23:27, 28).

In this damning image of the scribes and Pharisees, the Lord left us with an enigma. They prided themselves on being disciples of Moses from whom they had inherited all the teachings they were so justly proud of, and yet the Lord referred to their inheritance from the past as "dead men's bones." How then did the living law become transformed into dead men's bones? Was it because the law provided them with a skeletal structure of religion but without its lifeblood? The answer lies in what the Lord has already told us about these scribes and Pharisees.

They had replaced godliness, which was at the heart of the law, with the outward performance of religion. And in so doing, the inner qualities of the law became as dead men's bones. They had lost the sacred quality of a relationship with the living God enshrined in the words of Deuteronomy. "And now, Israel, what does the Lord your God require of you, but to fear the Lord your God, to walk in all His ways and to love Him, to serve the Lord your God with all your heart and with all your soul" (Deut. 10:12). The scribes and Pharisees, who would have known that injunction so well, chose to ignore it. What had been the living flesh of this commandment pulsing with life had become as dead men's bones.

To compound His condemnation, our Lord accused the scribes and Pharisees of a cover up, whether deliberate or not. He said they were like the whitewashing on the outside of a tomb, which was meant to distract the observer from the uncleanliness within. It was symbolic of the appearance of righteousness covering up the reality of hypocrisy and lawlessness.

In the Lord's words, there is a barbed truth. The scribes and Pharisees who prided themselves on their mastery of the law were, as the Lord asserted, lawless. The word Jesus used was *anomia*, which means a violation of law, non-observance or transgression of the law. They were hypocrites because their words and behavior gave the appearance of observing the law, but their inner reality before God told a different truth. No wonder they hated Jesus. It was a pretty bold accusation to hear out of the mouth of a carpenter's son from Nazareth.

The Lord's words apply to us today as well as all the people throughout the centuries. For wherever there is religion, there is always the possibility of dead men's bones. Religion is full of traditions, which provide the skeletal structure we pride ourselves on, but it can so easily take the place of a living relationship with our Lord and God. The unfortunate fact is that so many people today are unaware of these principles. Like the ancient scribes and Pharisees, people today pride themselves on a careful observance of the traditions of their fathers and equate their religious observances with piety.

The further unfortunate fact is that the Scriptures He has given us for our instruction incorporate all the truths related to godliness. In searching the Scriptures, we are in danger of missing the truths about the daily practice of love, mercy, faith, and hope, perhaps because we have not been taught otherwise. Will our ignorance incur the Lord's displeasure? May we pray every day for guidance.

The Eighth Woe

"Woe to you, scribes and Pharisees, hypocrites! Because you build the tombs of the prophets and adorn the monuments of the righteous, and say, 'If we had lived in the days of our fathers, we would not have been partakers with them in the blood of the prophets.' Therefore you are witnesses against yourselves that you are sons of those who murdered the prophets" (Matt. 23:29–31).

In His eighth indictment, the Lord reminded the scribes and Pharisees of another significant part of their religion. They built and adorned elaborate tombs for the prophets and the many righteous men who had died in the service of the Lord. It was as if they were declaring, "We are not guilty of their blood." And in building such edifices, they sought to shelter themselves from a share in the guilt of those who had killed them.

For the scribes and Pharisees, there was no penitence, either individual or collective. The Lord saw through their hypocrisy and reminded them that they were the sons of their fathers, and by denying any need to expresses penitence for their fathers' actions, they were also guilty by association. In place of penitence, there was arrogance fed by their achievements in building and adorning the tombs of the prophets.

Building and adorning the tombs of the prophets can arise out of a genuine desire to express reverence for those who have gone before. The house where Peter lived in Capernaum became a place of pilgrimage. The place where Peter died and where he was buried beneath the present Vatican had a wall inscribed by a pilgrim with the words *Petros ani*—"Peter is within" (William Steward McBirnie, *The Search for the Twelve Apostles* [Carol Stream, IL: Tyndale House Publishers, 2004], 45).

Such actions are a normal part of religious behavior, but where godliness is missing or poorly developed, men and women look for other things to fill that gap, and this is where hypocrisy comes to the forefront. It lies in the belief that an activity in the flesh, such as building and adorning the tombs of the fathers, is pleasing to God, while at the same time failing to live by faith in the living Lord.

Religion has been like this through the ages; men and women denying their personal responsibility for godliness and taking refuge in acts of religion that they mistakenly equate with godliness. On that day in Jerusalem, the Lord judged those who used their religion to deny responsibility. And so it will be in the future when we all stand before the judgment seat of Christ and have to answer for the deeds done in the name of our faith ... or perhaps in the name of our religion.

The Paradox

That last Tuesday before He died a criminal's death, the Lord did not only encounter men He called hypocrites, He also encountered a paradox enshrined in their lives. They had made it their life's work to study the Scriptures, for they thought that they could discover eternal life through their search, but the word translated "think," unlike the word "know," does not reflect certainty. It only suggests an unverified opinion. And Jesus put them straight when He told them that the Scriptures testified of Him. If they could find Him and build a relationship with the eternal Son of God, they would indeed find eternal life (see 1 John 5:12).

Their diligence is reflected in the Greek word *exereunao,* translated for "search," which means "to track and trace a matter as a lion tracks its prey, to search thoroughly by uncovering, to search minutely and explore a matter with diligence" (E. W. Bullinger, *A Critical Lexicon and Concordance* [London: Samuel Bagster and Sons, 1974], p. 672). In these matters they could not be faulted, and it is so in many churches and Bible study groups. The paradox is that even though they searched so carefully, they missed the truth. They found words, but not the One who authored the words.

In His Footsteps

On that Tuesday afternoon, my mind was mulling things over. I had searched the Scriptures all my Christian life, for I believed that I would find the truth that underpinned my faith. Was I in error? For how else could I explain the years of grey religion? I had been diligently observing all that I believed the Lord required of me in church and service and mission, but I had been doing so without the resounding song of joy I now know is my birthright as a child of the Father.

I heard His condemnation that day through parables and woes, and it was directed to those who seemed to have followed exactly the same path. Certainly the truth was there in the sacred writings, but what those Pharisees crowded around Him that day had missed was that there was a double truth embedded in the Scriptures. There was the truth of their faith embodied in the law and commandments, and the parallel truth that the God of all things longed for a deep and intimate relationship with those who searched the Scriptures.

I had learned what they had not. The relationship our mutual Father sought, longed for, and needed with His people had to be expressed in their love and faith. Perhaps they had indeed learned that God loved them, but their search had taken them no further than doctrine. They did not understand that He wanted them to venture out into the far deeper waters where they would trust Him with an unconditional and unreserved trust in all situations, and in that trust, abandon themselves to His Lordship. He stood with them that day in the temple, yet they did not recognize the One who longed for that relationship with them.

For me, the same caution applies today. I have to search the Scriptures so that I can find and master the principles that rule the kingdom of my Father. When I discover and apply those principles relating to repentance, confession, faith, prayer, and love, I will advance in my walk as His disciple and earn the approval of the One who was soon to die for me.

Chapter Seven
TUESDAY EVENING: When Shall These Things Be?

Introduction and Questions

That Tuesday evening Peter, James, John, and Andrew gathered around Him on the Mount of Olives (see Mark 13:3) and asked Him two questions. Matthew, Mark, and Luke record the Lord's answers. John omits them altogether (see Matt. 24:1–3; Mark 13:1–4; Luke 21:5–7). In this chapter I have dealt with each question as it relates to events in the Father's timetable for His church, His people, and for the whole world.

As the Lord left the temple for the last time, some of His disciples drew His attention to the beautiful stones of the temple, many of which were faced with gold. Matthew, Mark, and Luke record the disciples' questions though with variations. The Greek text says, "Tell us, when will these things be? And what will be the sign of Your coming, and of the end of the age?" (Matt. 24:3). Although many commentators divide the second question into two parts and treat them as two questions, it is important to note the specific elements in the disciples' words. The word "presence" is *parousia*. It is translated as "coming" in most versions, but it has a wider meaning. It can mean "being or becoming present, an arrival which includes the idea of coming to take up permanent residence" (Bullinger, p. 169).

An important word the disciples used in their questions is *kai*, which is translated "and." This refers to the connection of two things, ideas, or events that belong together. In this case the two events that the disciples connected, though they may not have understood the connection, were the sign of His coming and of the end of the age. Not two signs, only one, but signaling two events tied together in the plans of the Father for His people, the Jewish nation, and for the world.

The Lord's words to those four disciples on the Mount of Olives cover the period of time beginning with Pentecost and ending with the Lord's return. There is not enough space in this account for an inquiry into all of these events. But following is a brief overview of Jesus' response to His disciples concerning the end of the age.

The Fall of Jerusalem—AD 66–70

Luke 21:20–24 records Jesus' answer to their question about the stones of the temple not being left one on another. He began by telling them the sign of what was to come. "But when you see Jerusalem surrounded by armies, then know that its desolation is near" (Luke 21:20). The City of David was surrounded twice by Roman armies. The first encirclement took place in AD 66 after an unlikely coalition of Sadducees, Pharisees, Christians, and the Hasidim rebelled against Rome. The general in charge of the Roman armies, Cestius Gallus, surrounded Jerusalem, but he withdrew his forces unexpectedly.

This was the sign Jesus had predicted (Matt. 24:15–22). According to His instruction, the Christians living in Jerusalem escaped and fled the city when the Roman armies retreated.

When Titus arrived on the scene and surrounded the city in AD 70, it was the time of the Passover, and millions of Jews were in the city. Titus built a massive earth wall around the city. No one could get out. Those who attempted to escape, and many did, were captured and crucified on the earthen wall as a testimony to their foolishness. Hundreds of people were crucified every day on that earth wall within sight of the inhabitants of the city.

One night the battle erupted in full measure, and a firebrand was thrown into an apartment near the temple, which quickly spread and set the whole structure ablaze. The Roman troops rushed into the temple and slaughtered all those who had taken refuge there. As the fire raged, the building collapsed and no stone was left unturned, just as Jesus had predicted. It is reported that more than a million Jews perished.

The vengeance of the Romans was pitiless. Jerusalem was destroyed, and its people were dispersed across many nations. The Lord's pronouncement to His disciples was fulfilled, "And they will fall by the edge of the sword, and be led away captive into all nations. And Jerusalem will be trampled by the Gentiles until the times of the Gentiles are fulfilled" (Luke 21:24).

The Beginning of Sorrows—AD 70–Present

Early in His discourse, Jesus turned their attention to the age that was to come into being at Pentecost. We call it the "church age." There were two things He told us of which to be aware, and unfortunately, both are negative. Jesus then went on to detail elements of the time He called "the beginning of sorrows."

"Take heed that no one deceives you. For many will come in My name, saying, 'I am the Christ,' and will deceive many. And you will hear of wars and rumors of wars. See that you are not troubled; for all these things must come to pass, but the end is not yet" (Matt. 24:4–6).

It is a matter of historical record that from that evening on the Mount of Olives, there have been a number of Jewish men who claimed to be the Messiah. Simon Bar Kokhba, in the second century, claimed that he would lead the people of Israel to victory against the Romans. Other Israelites who have claimed to be the Messiah include Sabbetai Zevi, who lived in the seventeenth century, and Ya'akov (Jacob) Frank, who lived in the eighteenth century. Frank claimed to be the reincarnation of Sabbetai Zevi and was accepted by his followers as the Messiah.

The second thing Jesus told those four disciples about the church age was that there would be "wars and rumors of wars." The Greek word translated "war" does not equate with our modern concept of wars spanning nations and continents. The word He used was *polemos*, which refers to the tumult of a local war rather than a worldwide conflict.

Matthew records Jesus' words, "All these things must come to pass, but the end is not yet" (Matt. 24:6). Jesus then referred to these calamities as "the beginning of sorrows" (Matt. 24:8). The word He used, which is translated "sorrows," is *odin*, which refers to a throe, a pain, especially of a woman in labor (see Bullinger, p. 719). In the economy of the Father, these signs are the birth pains of a new age when the Messiah will come again.

Our Lord's words then leapt past the intermediate centuries following AD 70 and focused on the years much closer to the end of the age. He told them of nation rising against nation and kingdom against kingdom, which He associated with famines, pestilence (plagues), and earthquakes in various places (Luke calls them "great earthquakes"; see Luke 21:11).

The words Jesus used nearly two thousand years ago put us today in the center of the picture. We know that in our day, earthquakes are not only increasing in intensity but also in frequency. The world is beset by famine and pestilence as millions suffer, particularly across the African continent. There are also wars, nation against nation, and people group against people group, often times within one's own country. There can be little doubt that we are in the midst of the period Jesus called "the beginning of sorrows."

And yet, the sorrow, tribulation, and persecution of Christ's followers will not last forever. The outcome of the final conflict between God and Satan has been recorded in Scripture. Jesus shared with His disciples the signs of His coming and the assurance of His return:

> *For as the lightning comes from the east and flashes to the west, so also will the coming of the Son of Man be ... Immediately after the tribulation of those days the sun will be darkened, and the moon will not give its light; the stars will fall from heaven, and the powers of the heavens will be shaken. Then the sign of the Son of Man will appear in heaven, and then all the tribes of the earth will mourn, and they will see the Son of Man coming on the clouds of heaven with power and great glory.* (Matt. 24:27, 29, 30)

As the end of the world approaches, Christ's followers must remember that God has promised to "never leave [them] nor forsake [them]" (Heb. 13:5). Jesus assured His disciples, which includes believers today, "I am with you always, even to the end of the age" (Matt. 28:20).

In His Footsteps

I was bowed by the greatness and severity of the Lord's promises. When I reflected that evening on the Mount of Olives on what the Scriptures taught about that coming time of wrath, I had a profound sense of relief, knowing that I am a member of Christ's church, His bride, whom He will return for. Knowing this truth is beyond expression. That evening, I found myself looking forward with a great sense of wonder to a coming time when I, with all those whom He has purchased, will take part in the marriage ceremony of the Lamb.

I had to confess to myself and to Him that my understanding of His gospel was severely limited. I thought the gospel began and ended with my receiving His salvation. The concept of a coming age when He would rule the earth was there on the fringes of my mind, but I had never given it more space than that. I had to face the truth that my own part in His eternal purposes was minuscule, a fragment of thread woven into the eternal and infinite fabric of the Father's will.

Did I accept my own part in what He foretold? Humbly, yes! Was I prepared to meet my Lord in the air? That would be the challenge I would have to face every day for the remainder of my life as I made the daily choice to be like the wise virgins in the parable that the Lord taught, being ready to meet the Bridegroom at any moment, and taking up my cross and following Him.

Chapter Eight
WEDNESDAY: Your Father, the Devil

The Last Quiet Day

It was a Wednesday in our reckoning and only two days before His death. In the absence of unassailable records about that day, I believe He spent the time in quiet reflection either with His disciples or alone with the Father. Wednesday was like a day of Sabbath rest before the next day, Thursday, which could only end with His final steps to Golgotha. He may have been seeking rest with His disciples, but His enemies certainly were not.

Luke reports that the previous day the Lord had been teaching in the temple but that night had stayed on the Mount of Olives (see Luke 21:37). What took place there is hidden from us. Perhaps in the silence of His soul before His death, He spent the time in conversation with His Father. Perhaps in some quiet place He spoke with His disciples of His coming death. Perhaps they sought to be assured that He would not leave them. We won't know until we experience Jesus' return.

Luke also reports that the following morning the people came to the temple expecting to listen to Jesus teach (see Luke 21:38). But of that there is also no record. From the accounts of Matthew and Mark, we infer that His last public discourse took place in the temple and on the Mount of Olives on Tuesday. And from the silence of Matthew, Mark, and Luke, we assume that Wednesday was a day of rest for the Lord before the tumults of His last days.

But one thing was certain about that day. The chief priests and scribes were not silent, for they were actively seeking ways to destroy the One who had so publically exposed their hypocrisy. And there was another one who was active that day. The records tell us that on that day Judas' frustrations, because of his own aspirations about a coming kingdom, overwhelmed him. Those frustrations found common cause with the fear, hatred, and antagonism of the Jewish leaders as they worked to do the will of their own evil master. Between them all—Judas, the leaders of the Sanhedrin, Lucifer, and the Eternal Father—the decisions were made for the Son of the Father to be betrayed.

Lucifer

Lucifer, or Satan, had longed for this moment. As a created being in God's kingdom, Lucifer had enjoyed the blessings of the Father. He had served as a "covering cherub" (Ezek. 28:16, KJV), but he allowed pride and selfishness to infect him. Lucifer aspired to become like the Most High. Isaiah records that Satan said to himself: "I will ascend into heaven, I will exalt my throne above the stars [angels] of God; I will also sit on the mount of the congregation on the farthest sides of the north; I will ascend above the heights of the clouds, I will be like the Most High" (Isa. 14:13, 14). Through Judas and the Jewish leaders, Satan sought to destroy Christ and exalt himself.

The ancient Hebrew name for this evil one was translated into Greek using two different words: *satanas* (the adversary) and *diabolos* (the devil, the false accuser). The Hebrews knew him as the one who maligns the saints, who is always seeking to undermine the security of their walk with the Lord, and who is always opposed to the disciple's relationship with the Master. Today, we call him Satan.

He is a strand of evil lacing together the kingdoms of the world into a net to trap the unwary and to hold them captive at his will. He is an unfathomable pool of darkness; he is a black hole that will not admit light in the constellations of his earthly kingdoms. Those who fall into its malevolent depths are deluded about their plight and lose their will to see, understand, and seek the good.

He is a despot going where he will, always on the lookout for those who threaten to disrupt his rule. He is pride without grace and maintains a greed for power that can never be satisfied. He creates a lust for worship in his followers, who are promised everything and receive nothing unless it comes at a terrible price. He is a lie without repentance, deceit that bends every way without straightness, and condemnation without forgiveness. He is the opponent of all that is holy and good. He is incapable of righteousness and implacable in his hatred of the Lord and His saints. And his implacable desire is for all the elements of his character to be installed as the permanent furnishings of those who bend to his will.

The Lord called him Beelzebub, which could be translated as "the ruler of demons" (see Matt. 12:24), "an enemy" (see Matt. 13:28, 29), "the tempter" (see Matt. 4:3), "the wicked one" (see Matt. 13:19), and the father of lies (see John 8:44). Paul called him "the prince of the power of the air" (see Eph. 2:2). He was known to John the prophet as "Apollyon" (see Rev. 9:11).

Satan remained an exalted angelic being even though he fell. His character had embraced evil, but his status had not changed. The writer of the book of Job records that Satan twice came into heaven's throne room with other angels to present himself to the Lord.

Did Satan have access to the throne of God? Yes! Did he have permission to discuss the life of Job? Yes! Did he have the authority to command the Sabeans and then the Chaldeans to come and destroy Job's possessions as well as kill the saint's servants? Yes! Could the evil one command fire to fall from heaven? Yes! Could he call for the winds to destroy Job's house? Yes! Did he have the power to afflict Job with painful sores? Yes! But were there limitations on the power and authority of the evil one? Also, thankfully, *yes*!

Limitations for the devil were put in place by the decree of the Father Himself (see Job 1:12–19; 2:7). When asked by the Father where he had come from, Satan told the Father that he had been roaming the earth (see Job 1:7). Disciples of the Most High also live in Satan's world. It is his customary dwelling place, and he knows all the corners of its power and degradation with the utmost familiarity. We delude ourselves if we think otherwise and instead imagine that the part of the world we inhabit is exempt from his evil.

Peter reminds us that Satan is looking for someone to devour (see 1 Peter 5:8). The word "devour" means "to drink down, to swallow down, to swallow up" (Bullinger, p. 223). Peter used an image of the lion's prey losing its identity after being swallowed and digested in the lion's stomach. It became one with its tormentor and absorbed into his being. This is an apt description of what Satan intends for all the followers of our Lord. He is not just opposing the Lord's disciples in the twenty-first century. He is compulsively committed to devouring them, make them captive in his own evil ways, and there render them powerless so that the evil of his own kingdom will predominate.

On the Lord's last Wednesday, Satan began to muster those who owed their allegiance to him. One of those enemies was Judas in whom a devil lived. Another enemy was made up of those who prized religion above godliness, if indeed they understood godliness. Jesus confronted the leaders of the Jews with a most damning denunciation, "You are of your father the devil, and the desires of your father you want to do. He was a murderer from the beginning, and does not stand in the truth, because there is no truth in him. When he speaks a lie, he speaks from his own resources, for he is a liar and the father of it" (John 8:44).

That fatal Wednesday Satan called together his own resources; he brought all the liars like himself, and in their anger and hatred, they were also murderers like the one who had been a murderer from the beginning. The leaders of the Jews were ready, for they wanted to kill the Messiah. Then there was Judas, who had a key role to play in the machinations of the Lord's enemies. And together, these three enemies gathered and began to play their own parts in the coming betrayal and death of the Messiah and of Jesus our Lord.

Leaders of the Jews

There were so many of them, but they were not a coherent group. However, there was one thing they all had in common in those last days of the Lord's life among men. They hated and feared Him. In the beginning these aggravated emotions had not yet had time to develop, for He was only the rabbi from Nazareth.

Early in His first year of public ministry, He had come to Jerusalem and there forcibly propelled Himself into their attention with an act that struck at their extensive financial interests. John reports that Jesus drove the animals and money changers from the temple with a whip, knocking over their tables and commanding the sellers of doves to take the birds out of the temple. In a firm voice, He reminded everyone who was listening that His Father's house was not meant to be a marketplace (see John 2:14–16).

During that visit to Jerusalem for Passover, as John reports, "many believed in His name when they saw the signs which He did" (John 2:23). There are no records of active opposition from the leaders of the Jews during this first visit to the holy city. But one can well imagine the lengthy discussions that went on in the Sanhedrin, the supreme Jewish governing body, about this wandering rabbi. He had struck at their financial interests (the chief priests had a well-established stake in all the temple transactions), and His miracles pointed to a greater authority than theirs.

The Sanhedrin was made up of seventy-one members and was dominated by a priestly aristocracy of Sadducees. The Sanhedrin also included scribes, who were teaching lawyers, as well as members of the closed community of Pharisees. But the group with the most power in the Sanhedrin were the chief priests, including those actively serving in the temple and those who had previously served in that office. These were the ones with extensive financial interests in the market operations in the temple. And because this group had political, religious, and financial interests, they had the most to lose if the people believed Jesus' teachings. Their opposition was relatively quiet during our Lord's first year, which has been called the year of inauguration.

His second year, during which His popularity grew, was spent mainly in Galilee with one exception: His second visit to Jerusalem for the Passover. At that time He again came to the attention of the Jewish leaders when a cripple was healed at the pool of Bethesda (see John 5:1–16). They might have dismissed that miracle but for one thing that struck at the heart of their religious power and their control over the people. Jesus healed the cripple on the Sabbath. Then as John again reports, the anger of the Jews welled up so that they persecuted Him and looked for ways to kill Him (see John 5:16).

Now their opposition had another focus that they added to their anger about Jesus overturning the money changers' tables. The Sabbath was sacred, and the scribes had erected a formidable array of teachings to impose religious observance of the Sabbath on the general populace. No work could be done. No meals could be cooked, no repairs made to a torn garment, no herbs picked for food, no flowers cut for adornment, and the only journey that was permitted was one that took a thousand double paces from the point of residence. The miracle at the pool of Bethesda on the Sabbath, when no work was to be done, struck at the heart of their religious control.

The opposition of the Jewish leaders to Jesus during that second year, His year of popularity, reached its peak during the third year, which has been called the year of opposition. And that brings us to the last week of our Lord's life among men. As we have seen, His footsteps to Golgotha took Him again into the temple where His acts again compounded the anger of the Jewish leaders. He drove out the money changers and those who made His house of prayer a house of merchandise and profit. His acts forcibly reminded the Jewish leaders of His opposition to their established religious practices and His contempt for the things they held most sacred.

The previous day the Lord had condemned them when He pronounced eight woes against their hypocrisy. Their hatred and fear of Him had now come to a crescendo, for they knew He stood against all that they valued. Now all that they needed before they could put Him to death was someone who would betray Him. Then Judas came.

Judas

He was probably born in the town of Kerioth in Judea. If this is so, then his name, Judas Iscariot, simply means that he was Judas from Kerioth. He, being Judean, was the odd man out in a company of disciples who were all Galileans. Why then did he agree to join such a select band? The answer is hidden, and we can only speculate because the Scriptures are silent.

Like many Jews who suffered under the tyranny of the Romans, he found relief from that tyranny in the belief that the Messiah would come, and with Him, the restoration of the kingdom. One can imagine the excitement in Bethabara beyond the Jordan when Andrew told Simon that they had found the Messiah (see John 1:41).

Judas would most certainly have accepted that Jesus of Nazareth was their Messiah, and this was perhaps the first reason for him joining the disciples. Then as the days lengthened into months and then into years, and he found that the One he had pinned his hopes on was going to die, his belief in Jesus the Messiah would have faded into disillusionment. From there, it was an easy step to betrayal.

The second reason Judas may have agreed to join that select band was embedded in his contrary and often confused character. This would only emerge later when his true character became known. After Mary had poured out her ointment on the Lord's body, Judas protested that the ointment could have been sold, and the money could have been given to the poor. John reports, "This he said, not that he cared for the poor, but because he was a thief, and had the money box; and he used to take what was put in it" (John 12:6).

We don't know what Judas left behind when he became a disciple, but it is clear that he wasn't going to be disadvantaged by following Jesus. And having charge of the funds was an easy way to place his interests before those of the One he supposedly followed.

The third reason for his membership in the company of twelve would not have been clear to anyone but the Lord, for He understood the character of Judas even before He called him. While He was in Galilee, John reports, "Jesus answered them, 'Did I not choose you, the twelve, and one of you is a devil?' He spoke of Judas Iscariot, the son of Simon, for it was he who would betray Him, being one of the twelve" (John 6:70, 71). The word "devil" that Jesus used to describe Judas was originally *diabolos*, which is the same word Jesus used when He spoke of His archenemy, Satan (see John 8:44; 13:2).

Why did Jesus allow Judas, a man in whom a devil lived, to become one of His disciples? Because it was part of the Father's plan. The question takes us deep into the mysteries of our Father's purposes. The Father placed among His Son's disciples the one person He knew would betray Him. The final days of Jesus' life among men—the betrayal, the trials, the scourging, and then the dishonorable death were as sure as the sunrise. And one has to note that everything Jesus said and did, as directed by the Father, would have been reported to the prince of devils by the demon who lived in Judas.

On that last Wednesday when Jesus and His disciples rested on the Mount of Olives, Judas was hard at work. Taking his frustrations and disillusionments with him, he went to the chief priests as both Matthew and Mark report. I have combined their reports to give the sequence of what happened that day in the temple precincts:

Then Judas Iscariot, one of the twelve, went to the chief priests to betray Him, and said, "What are you willing to give me if I deliver Him to you?" (see Matt. 26:14, 15). When they heard it they were glad and promised to give him money. And they counted out to him thirty pieces of silver (see Mark 14:10, 11). Judas then sought how he might conveniently betray Him (see Matt. 26:16).

After that dishonorable contract with the leaders of the Jews, Judas would have rejoined the disciples, for he was with them when they met the next day in the upper room. We don't know where they spent the night. Perhaps they slept on the Mount of Olives or in the home of Martha, Mary, and Lazarus. There are no records, but the stage was set. The actors were in place. When Thursday dawned, Jesus, knowing that His end was so very near, sent two disciples ahead to prepare for the Passover meal.

In His Footsteps

Knowing that there were so many arrayed against Him and knowing that the terrible death by crucifixion lay just hours away, the Lord chose to spend that day in silent rest. I would have been frantically busy looking for a way out, but if I had done so, I would have missed that most important truth that the writer to the Hebrews spoke about. He affirmed that there was a rest for the people of God, for those who entered this rest had forsaken their own works. The writer then drew a parallel between the disciple's rest and God resting from His own works on the Sabbath day (see Heb. 4:9, 10).

I know that rest now. I did not know it when I sought Him out on the Mount of Olives, but it is sure that my Lord was at rest that Wednesday before His betrayal. He had ceased from His own works on the way to Golgotha as surely as God had on the seventh day. My Lord's rest was in obvious counterpoint to the restless energies of those who would have Him killed. And that is always the way of those who face against our Lord and seek to obstruct, knowingly or unknowingly, the will and ways of the Father expressed in His children.

In bowing to the Father's will, as He had done all His life, my Lord laid down a pattern for me and for all of us across the centuries who would seek the Lord's approval. Cease from my own works. Cut short and lay to rest my restless energies. Stop trying to arrange everything in the orbit of my world. Stop carrying out the works that will bring the desires of my flesh to their ungainly conclusions. Refuse to order my life in the image of all those who also live around me in this world. They are not the pattern for my life. He is.

In resting that day on the Mount of Olives, I found the same contentment my Lord had. This was not a contentment based on the outcomes of my own energies but was rather a contentment securely based on the twin pillars of His faith and my faith; His trust, and therefore my trust, in the Father that He would do as He had planned from the foundation of the world, and His obedience, hence my obedience, to the Father so that His will might be done on earth. And so His last Wednesday came to an end. His footsteps to Golgotha were nearly at an end.

Chapter Nine
THURSDAY: I Have Desired to Eat This Passover

Introduction

Thursday began with the Lord rested after His last sleep. And there would be no more rest until the silence of death closed around Him on the cross. His footsteps to Golgotha were nearly at an end. All that remained was the last meal with His disciples, which would also be the first meal that opened the doors into the coming church. There was still so much more to do. On this final Thursday, His footsteps would take Him to the upper room. There, He would eat His final meal with His disciples and then cross the Kidron Valley into Gethsemane. Beyond that, the unspeakable horrors of His last hours waited for the Son of the living God.

Prepare the Passover

The record provided by Matthew, Mark, and Luke begins with Jesus and His disciples somewhere outside the city. We don't know where, perhaps Bethany or the Mount of Olives. The time had come for them to eat the Passover meal, so Jesus sent Peter and John into the city with instructions to find a man, probably a servant, bearing a pitcher of water. They were to follow him to his house and there give the master of the house this message, "The Teacher says, 'My time is at hand; I will keep the Passover at your house with My disciples'" (Matt. 26:18). Luke records the Lord's words to the master of the house slightly differently. He wrote, "The Teacher says to you, 'Where is the guest room where I may eat the Passover with My disciples?'" (Luke 22:11). We note that the master of the house would have been a disciple of our Lord, for the Lord called Himself the teacher; this was not the word used in public discourse, which was rabbi.

We also note that Jesus asked for the guest room, the *kataluma*, which was also the designation of the humble place where Jesus was born. This was an open place, often without a roof where animals were unloaded, shoes and staff and dusty garments were put off, where straw for animals was stored, where fires could be lit and people could cook and eat. It is a humbling recognition that in the last hours of His life, Jesus recognised His humble beginnings and acknowledged that He could end His relationships with His disciples in the same manner.

The Lord then told Peter and John that the master of the house would show them a large furnished upper room where they were to prepare for the Passover. The Lord spoke privately with Peter and John, for, I believe, the Lord understood that Judas had planned His betrayal, and He refused to give him the satisfaction of knowing where He would spend His final hours.

Peter and John found the servant with the water jar, went to the house, and spoke with the master, who showed them the upper room with its tables arranged in a deep U. What the records do not tell us is how Peter and John prepared for the Passover. However, with the help of such biblical scholars as Alfred Edersheim, we are able to imagine what probably happened based on the cultural rites of the day.

During the morning of that final Thursday, Peter and John went to the temple where the Passover lamb, one of many, was killed, and its blood poured on the base of the altar. The Levites chanted the "Hallel" from Psalms 113–118 with the people responding with the shouted praise, "Hallelujah." Peter and John would have then carried the slaughtered lamb back to the house where they would eat the Passover. In the courtyard of that house, the lamb was roasted, according to tradition, on a pomegranate spit and when cooked, placed on a small table and taken to the upper room. There the lamb was placed with the unfermented wine, three unleavened cakes stacked on top of each other, bitter herbs, and a dish of vinegar. Peter and John then rejoined Jesus and the company of disciples, including Judas.

Around midafternoon, the full company returned to the city to the house where all had been made ready and entered the upper room. The Passover meal could now begin.

The Dispute

The gospel writers omit most of the details of the Passover meal, but from other reliable records, we are able to construct a probable sequence of events that began with an argument.

They entered the upper room, probably up the stairs from the street, on the outside of the house and immediately began to argue about who was the greatest among them. The U shaped arrangements of the table and cushions required that someone had to decide who was to occupy the favored place on the left of the Master. This spot was traditionally reserved for the one who was the greatest among them and that led to a dispute about who was the greater. The one who was greatest would be seated at the Lord's left hand, and the one who was least would take the place at the opposite end of the table.

We can't be entirely sure what had set that dispute in motion, but we do know about our Lord's gentle chiding of His beloved and fractious disciples. Speaking of the exercise of lordship among the Gentiles, He told them in words that also applied to Himself that those who would be the greatest among His disciples had to be as a servant to others (see Luke 22:26).

This unseemly dispute may have been the trigger for Peter to retreat to the far end of the second table opposite John and to take the place of least honor. And the place of honor was taken by the one least qualified to sit at the Lord's left hand: Judas, the betrayer in whom Satan had found a dwelling place.

Washing the Disciples' Feet

As the disciples reclined around the table with Jesus, He spoke words that focused their attention on both the present and the future. "With fervent desire I have desired to eat this Passover with you before I suffer; for I say to you, I will no longer eat of it until it is fulfilled in the kingdom of God" (Luke 22:15, 16).

In these words Jesus our Lord was both present Teacher and future King, pointing to the outcomes the Father would achieve at the end of His footsteps to Golgotha. He would experience death by crucifixion to bear the sin of the world; then He would resurrect and ascend to the Father.

Before the feast began, Jesus rose, took off His outer garment, and wrapped a towel around His waist. He then poured water into a basin and started to wash the disciples' feet (see John 13:4, 5). The disciples would have been shocked, not simply because the One they followed had chosen to wash their feet, but that He also had taken the towel used by the lowest of slaves in order to perform a duty that only slaves performed.

In that act our Lord expressed the sharp radical difference between the contentious ways of the world that were expressed in their dispute, and the ways of His kingdom where greatness was measured by humility and service. And our Lord, whom we know as the Creator of heaven and earth, told them that He was among them as One who served (see Luke 22:27).

Peter impulsively refused the offer, saying, "'You shall never wash my feet!' Jesus answered him, 'If I do not wash you, you have no part with Me.' Simon Peter said to Him, 'Lord, not my feet only, but also my hands and my head!'" (John 13:8, 9).

At that time, Peter did not understand the act of service. It was alien to him, and he could not yet comprehend what Jesus had done. It wasn't until Pentecost when the Holy Spirit transformed his mind that he began his spiritual journey of renewal.

The Passover

A traditional Passover meal begins with offering a blessing over the cup and sharing the drink with those around the table. Jesus "took the cup, and gave thanks, and said, 'Take this and divide it among yourselves; for I say to you, I will not drink of the fruit of the vine until the kingdom of God comes'" (Luke 22:17, 18).

Symbolism was an integral part of the Passover. The various parts of the meal reminded the Jews of the life of their people in Egypt and their delivery from bitter bondage. According to Jewish culture, after offering a blessing over the unfermented wine and the washing of the hands, a vegetable, usually parsley, was dipped in salt and eaten. Following that, tradition stated that one of the three *matzahs* (unleavened bread) was broken.

At this time in the Passover meal, per tradition, Jesus may have related the story of the exodus and how the Israelites chose a lamb or goat, killed it, and sprinkled its blood on the doorposts and lintel so that the angel of death would pass over that house. The Lord knew what that meant, as John the Baptist had declared beyond Jordan, He was "the Lamb of God who takes away the sin of the world" (John 1:29). And soon He would bring that image of the lamb slain out of the cloisters of history into the real light of an eternal day. They would have drunk the second cup of unfermented wine and ritually washed their hands in preparation of eating the unleavened bread with bitter herbs and *charoset*, a sweet paste of nuts and apples symbolizing the mortar used by the slaves in Egypt.

The Betrayer

As the meal progressed, another drama was unfolding in the upper room, beginning with a very brief dialogue between the Lord and His betrayer, whom the Lord had identified with the words, "I do not speak concerning all of you. I know whom I have chosen; but that the Scripture may be fulfilled, 'He who eats bread with Me has lifted up his heel against Me'" (John 13:18; see Ps. 41:9). John then reports, "When Jesus had said these things, He was troubled in spirit" (John 13:21).

"Troubled" refers to the Lord being stirred up with conflicting emotions, as He dealt with both His love for Judas and His grief that one He had trusted would betray Him. The Lord then added, "Most assuredly, I say to you, one of you will betray Me" (John 13:21). And He knew who that would be; He had even known before He had chosen Judas (see John 6:70). For it had been ordained in the councils of heaven that

His betrayal would be by one who had walked with Him in the intimate company of those He had chosen; the betrayer would be one who would desert the Lord's love and trust.

At this point in the meal, the disciples were perplexed as they wondered who the Lord had meant. After a prompting from Peter, John asked Jesus whom he was talking about (see John 13:22–25).

"Jesus answered, 'It is he to whom I shall give a piece of bread when I have dipped it.' And having dipped the bread, He gave it to Judas Iscariot, the son of Simon. Now after the piece of bread, Satan entered him. Then Jesus said to him, 'What you do, do quickly'" (John 13:26, 27). John reports that Judas went out and that it was night (see John 13:30).

Darkness, the darkness of Satan, was in Judas' soul. Judas had entertained darkness, and it had overtaken and wrapped him in its poisonous and destructive web. When Judas left to accomplish his mission for the high priests of betraying Jesus, I believe that light returned to the upper room, and Jesus and His disciples could attend to the remainder of the meal, in which Jesus shared precious truths with His followers before His death.

"And as they were eating, Jesus took bread, blessed and broke it, and gave it to them and said, 'Take, eat; this is My body.' Then He took the cup, and when He had given thanks He gave it to them, and they all drank from it. And He said to them, 'This is My blood of the new covenant, which is shed for many. Assuredly, I say to you, I will no longer drink of the fruit of the vine until that day when I drink it new in the kingdom of God'" (Mark 14:22–25).

After that the disciples sang a hymn and left the upper room and made their way to the Mount of Olives (Mark 14:26).

Love One Another

As they walked, Jesus continued to instruct His disciples, "Little children, I shall be with you a little while longer. You will seek Me; and as I said to the Jews, 'Where I am going, you cannot come,' so I now say to you" (John 13:33). He then reminded them of a principle that would forever govern their lives and the lives of all who follow Him down through the ages. "A new commandment I give to you, that you love one another; as I have loved you, that you also love one another. By this all will know that you are My disciples, if you have love for one another" (John 13:34, 35).

Most of us are familiar with the word Jesus used to describe the essence of His relationship with His disciples. It is *agape* and has a meaning not found in classical Greek. It refers to "the love which springs from admiration amounting to veneration and respect for the other person however unlovely, which makes loving an act of choice, and which expresses that love in self denial" (Bullinger, p. 469).

Nothing could more accurately express the Lord's love, the Father's love, and the love of the Holy Spirit for those disciples in Jerusalem and for all of us down through the ages. And I am confounded, for there is nothing in me or in any of us that could claim that kind of love apart from His most gracious favor. In that commandment Jesus committed Himself to loving those who through the centuries would follow Him.

Peter's Protest

The unpredictable side of humanity's nature then emerged with Peter protesting, "Lord, why cannot I follow You now? I will lay down my life for Your sake" (John 13:37). But the Lord knew His often unpredictable and volatile servant so well. He knew what would follow in the palace of the high priest and then told His fractious disciple that he would deny his Lord three times before the rooster crowed (see John 13:38). Peter does not respond to the Lord's prediction, yet the impact on his heart must have been profound. It must have created incredible confusion between his own desire to be loyal to his Lord, and Jesus' prediction, which had he been listening, would have revealed to Peter so much of his unstable temperament.

The Lord's Supper

Paul, in his first letter to Corinthians, addresses the institution of the Lord's Supper: "For I received from the Lord that which I also delivered to you: that the Lord Jesus, on the same night in which He was betrayed took bread [the remaining piece of *matzah*]; and when He had given thanks, He broke it and said, 'Take, eat; this is My body, which is broken for you; do this in remembrance of Me'" (1 Cor. 11:23, 24).

Paul goes on to say, "In the same way He took the [third] cup also after supper, saying, 'This cup is the new covenant in My blood. This do, as often as you drink it, in remembrance of Me" (1 Cor. 11:25). The following day the cup of His blood was indeed poured out and the covenant He promised was ratified forever.

The word "covenant" can be defined as an agreement willingly entered into by two parties. The first party in the covenant is the Lord, who holds out the promise of forgiveness and of eternal life. This truth also confounds me. From birth, I have been a sinner so that every sin I have ever committed claims its just reward, which is death in both its physical and spiritual forms (see Rom. 6:23). So why should the Most Holy One want to enter a covenant with me? The truth is that He loves me and even that truth confounds me.

On the other hand, when I hear the Spirit's call to repentance and confession of the embarrassing facts of my sins, which I have long guarded as my own special possession, my impossible debt is forgiven. I take great comfort from the psalmist's words that God has removed my sins and cast them as far as the east is from the west, which is an infinite distance (see Ps. 103:12). And as the prophet wrote when speaking of the children of Israel and of our God down through the ages, "For I will forgive their iniquity, and their sin I will remember no more" (Jer. 31:34). And when my debt has been forgiven and that forgiveness accepted as His supreme gift to me, His Spirit tells my spirit that I am part of His family, and I can honestly call Him "Abba, Father" (Rom. 8:15) with all my heart.

When these facts of the Gospel are in place, I embrace the covenant He established that night and ratified the next day between two thieves. That same blood cleanses me, and my walk into eternity has begun.

In the upper room that night Jesus gave His disciples and all of us symbols of His great sacrifice. As Paul wrote in his first letter to the *ekklesia* (church) at Corinth, "For as often as you eat this bread and drink this cup, you proclaim the Lord's death till He comes" (1 Cor. 11:26). The Lord's Supper is to be a reminder of Jesus' gift and the promise of His return.

What the Lord made simple that night, humanity has complicated. Down through the ages, churches have replaced the simple ceremony with so many doctrines and rituals. Some people teach that you cannot be forgiven without this ritual or that you remain locked in your sins if you do not partake in communion. I wonder whether the grief the Lord experienced that evening over Judas' betrayal has been compounded over the centuries by the waywardness of people straying from the simplicity of what the Lord bestowed on His church—an act of remembrance of His gift and His return.

In His Footsteps

It is presumptuous to write as though I was there in that upper room, hiding away unobtrusively in a darkened corner and listening to all that was said. Yet events that took place and words that were spoken that night are securely lodged in my heart and will remain there forever.

I heard Peter's protestations about not forsaking Him and wondered how accurately that described my own sometimes uncertain walk with the Master. I heard the Master telling Peter that Satan had desired to have him, so he might sift him as wheat; it caused me to wonder at the savagery of those words. I knew that the Lord's words, "desired to have you," could well be translated that Satan "begged the Father earnestly and aggressively to have Peter for himself, that he might sift him as wheat."

The word "sift" could be explained as to shake continually so that the good and the worthless parts of the grain are separated.

I wondered whether the Lord's adversary had overstepped himself. The purpose of sifting was indeed to separate the grain from the chaff. But the chaff was always blown away while the grain remained. The net effect of Peter's trials would certainly be a savage sifting that the adversary engineered, but the rubbish in his life, which made it possible for the adversary to try for a claim on Peter's life, would be blown away. And in answer to the Lord's prayer, the whole grain, Peter's faith, would remain, and he would be better because of the sifting and sorting (see Luke 22:31–34).

Hiding away in a corner of that room, I wondered about how accurately the Lord had described the mixture in my own life. The chaff of the energies of my old nature that I needed to be rid of were mixed with my capacity for trust in the One who was soon to die. And what would it take for those two elements in my life, the grain and the chaff, to be separated? Would I have to wait for the adversary to give me his unwelcome attention? Or would I be able, with the Spirit's involvement, to attend to that sifting myself, apart from what the adversary could engineer?

I reserved those questions for a future time when I had mastered, if I ever could, what it meant to take up my cross and follow Him. I knew I needed far more than my very restricted human nature if I was ever to live out the answer to my questions. Then we left the upper room and began the next part of our journey to the cross.

Chapter Ten
THURSDAY: I Will Not Leave You Orphans

Introduction
Chapters fourteen, fifteen, and sixteen of John's gospel contain a number of teachings that are essential to life as His disciple, while chapter seventeen is devoted to the Lord's own prayer to His Father. These teachings and prayer are sandwiched between records of the Passover meal and of His agony in the Garden of Gethsemane. It is safe to assume that all took place either at the table or in the house where they celebrated Passover and before they left to cross the Kidron Valley into the darkness of the olive grove. I have arranged these teachings in thematic rather than in chronological order, grouping similar teachings into one cohesive statement.

Preparation of the Bride
After they had eaten the Passover, the Lord gave them a promise that would anchor the rest of His teaching, "In My Father's house are many mansions: if it were not so, I would have told you. I go to prepare a place for you. And if I go and prepare a place for you, I will come again and receive you to Myself; that where I am, there you may be also" (John 14:2, 3).

For so many who take the Scriptures out of context, this is read as a promise to individuals, but that interpretation needs to be carefully examined. The word "you," which Jesus used five times in these two verses, is plural, referring to each disciple individually but also to their identity as a collective unit. He was speaking beyond Pentecost when the plural "you" would be expressed in the title that has resounded through the ages. Our Lord was referring to His beloved church.

His church is known by a number of names: the body of Christ, the *ekklesia*, and the bride of Christ. The last title takes us into the center of Jewish tradition, which His disciples would have all understood.

It was the image of the bridegroom leaving his betrothed after their betrothal to go and prepare the house where they would live together. According to Jewish custom, this separation between the bridegroom and his bride could take as much as a year, during which time there would be no physical contact between them.

As He spoke with His disciples that night, Jesus knew that in a very short while their Bridegroom would leave them. They would see the resurrected Lord being lifted up into the clouds to the Father, and then the two angels would tell them that He would come again as they had seen Him go (see Acts 1:11). There in the upper room He referred to the same theme. "I will come again and receive you to Myself; that where I am, there you may be also" (John 14:3).

The image of the bride and groom was not a strange doctrine in biblical terms. John the Baptist spoke about Jesus to a number of Jews and referred to Him as the Bridegroom (see John 3:29). John did not explain who the bride was, but there was no doubt in his mind that Jesus was the Bridegroom.

This image of the bride-to-be after her betrothal and the One who will be her husband is picked up by Paul in his second letter to the *ekklesia* at Corinth, "For I have betrothed you to one husband, that I may present you [the church] as a chaste virgin to Christ" (2 Cor. 11:2).

According to Jewish tradition, which the disciples, both married and unmarried all understood, the Bridegroom left the one to whom He was betrothed to go and prepare their joint dwelling place. He then promised to return to earth to receive His bride to Himself and to take her to the dwelling place He had prepared for both of them. It is important to note that the Lord used the Greek word translated as "mansions," but it can also be translated as "dwelling places." It is plural, but the word translated for "place" is singular. Many dwelling places in heaven, but there will be only one place where, according to Jewish tradition, He would take His church, so that He and His bride could dwell together forever.

Paul referred to the meeting of the Lord and His betrothed when he wrote to the *ekklesia* at Thessalonica.

> *For the Lord Himself will descend from heaven with a shout, with the voice of an archangel, and with the trumpet of God. And the dead in Christ will rise first. Then we who are alive and remain shall be caught up together with them in the clouds to meet the Lord in the air. And thus we [His church, His bride] shall always be with the Lord.* (1 Thess. 4:16, 17).

But that is not the end of the story. As with all Jewish marriages, after the

Bridegroom returns to receive His bride, the marriage feast follows. And John reports this extraordinary event, in words the Bridegroom Himself inspired through His Spirit. "Let us be glad and rejoice and give Him glory, for the marriage of the Lamb has come, and His wife has made herself ready. And to her it was granted to be arrayed in fine linen, clean and bright, for the fine linen is the righteous acts of the saints" (Rev. 19:7, 8).

That night in the upper room the disciples may not have fully grasped the importance of what the Lord had promised. Only as the Spirit filled and inspired them after Pentecost would the full truth of what awaited them be understood. For they would become the church, and the church was the bride of Christ. And the key to their transformation from a group of disciples united only through their being with Jesus, into the chosen *ekklesia* of God was the One who Jesus promised that night: the Holy Spirit of God, who would unite them into one body.

His Farewell Promise

He knew they were grieving. He knew when He spoke with them at the table that night that their hearts were troubled by His coming execution, so he said, "Let not your heart be troubled" (John 14:1). He understood their coming grief, as He does with all of us (see Heb. 4:15). He also told them, "I will not leave you orphans; I will come to you" (John 14:18) and also, "You have heard Me say to you, 'I am going away and coming back to you'" (John 14:28).

The word they all heard in their perhaps unbelieving ears was literally "I am coming to you," and a little over fifty days would elapse before He would fulfil His promise. He would not come in His renewed spiritual body, which would ascend to the Father. He would come in the Person of His own Spirit, the One we know as the Spirit of God and the Spirit of Christ. At that time His disciples would no longer be orphans and comfortless, but a whole new world would be opened to them.

That night He would not have them ignorant of what would happen at Pentecost, so on three occasions before Gethsemane, He spoke of the One who would come, telling them that He would ask the Father to send them the eternal Helper, who would soon live in them (see John 14:16, 17).

Jesus introduced His disciples to one of the most profound mysteries of His kingdom. The One who was agent of all creation was the same One who had been with them on their long journeys across the Promised Land, and now He would come and make His home within each of those disciples. The Lord needed His future bride to be about His Father's business while He was absent, and for that reason the Holy Spirit was sent to equip His body for the works ordained by the Father.

That night the Lord promised them that the Holy Spirit of God would teach them all things and bring to their minds all that Jesus had told them. They would remember every word, all the sacred principles of the kingdom, each of His commandments, every insight into our redeemed natures, and every instruction about following Him wherever He would lead them (see John 14:26). In that same place, Jesus told them that the Holy Spirit would lead them into all truth (see John 16:13). All things! All truth! Profound mysteries. For nothing in all our individual affairs, in the affairs of the church, and in the affairs of the whole world could ever be hidden from Him.

But the greatest mystery of all was not revealed by the Lord that night, but was the subject of inspired words given by the Holy Spirit to Paul some years later, "The love of God has been poured out in our hearts by the Holy Spirit who was given to us" (Rom. 5:5). Poured out! The Greek words Paul used are the same used to describe how the Lord poured out His life unto death on the cross (see Luke 22:20). Without stint. Beyond any measure humanity could devise. Poured out without holding back. His blood poured out on the cross so that His love could be poured out into our hearts.

But there is a second part to this mystery, which confounds all of us who shelter in its promises. That same night Jesus spoke of the love that the Holy Spirit would pour out into the hearts of His disciples, He also told them: "He who has My commandments and keeps them, it is he who loves Me. And he who loves Me will be loved by My Father, and I will love him and manifest Myself to him.... If anyone loves Me, he will keep My word; and My Father will love him, and We will come to him and make Our home with him" (John 14:21, 23).

The love Jesus spoke about is beyond the love that humanity is capable of experiencing. It is divine love, eternal love, love beyond understanding that links each of us and His church in an enduring bond, which will survive beyond time and into the far distant reaches of eternity. Jesus used the word *agape* to identify the love "which springs from admiration and veneration, which chooses the one to love with a deliberate decision of the will, and then devotes a self-denying and compassionate devotion to that person" (Bullinger, p. 469).

How could that be? I can understand how my love for Him would fall into that framework, but His love for me? Surely, that is impossible, but Jesus tells us otherwise. The Father and my own Lord as well as the Holy Spirit, each love me with the love that characterizes their own Persons. They admire, respect, and venerate me, but that is not all, for the Trinity devote Themselves to a self-denying devotion to me.

This God of ours confounds me. Confounded and humbled and in awe of Him as those first disciples were in awe as they watched their Lord at work in Jerusalem. But the mystery is compounded by the Lord's words: "and We will come to him and make Our home with him."

My walk in the footsteps of my Lord to Golgotha comes to an impassable chasm: the impassable gulf between our God and me. And as my feet stagger on this near side I know so well, I hear the Lord's extraordinary promise. He is not on the other side of the chasm with the Father and His Spirit. He is on my side. I don't have to cross over. They have done it in my place, for Father, Son, and Holy Spirit have come to make their dwelling place in me on my side of the chasm.

That is what their *agape* love is all about. When the Lord came to earth in *agape* love for all of us, He denied His divinity so that he could serve us, leaving behind all the glory of His eternal home with the Father and making Himself a servant and then dying for all of us (see Phil. 2:8).

That was the cost that purchased this extraordinary promise, for *agape* carries in its eternal embrace the fact that, as He denied Himself to serve humankind, so He continues to serve those of us who love Him with that same *agape* love poured out into our hearts by the Holy Spirit.

The Vine

The mystery deepened when the Lord took His disciples into another dimension of the Father's purposes. The mystery of the Father, Son, and the Holy Spirit making their home in me and with me was His opening idea of Him being the Vine and we being the branches. This is not only a static relationship of Him being in me and me being in Him, but a dynamic relationship with its own special meaning and purpose.

He told them, "I am the true vine, and My Father is the vinedresser.... As the branch cannot bear fruit of itself, unless it abides in the vine, neither can you, unless you abide in Me. I am the vine, you are the branches" (John 15:1, 4, 5). Now the relationship between each of us as members of His church takes on an active and dynamic quality. Each branch is an extension of the Vine itself. The life of the Vine flows through each branch so that the quality of life of the Vine will be expressed in the fruit that each branch bears.

This image of a life in common. Vine and branches begs the question: how are we to understand the life of the Vine we all share? And here I must confess an initial ignorance of these very special meanings. At first I thought that what I had received when I first believed was a life that would live forever. My new eternal life began the moment I believed and would take me across the threshold through the gateway into heaven, and my life that would go on forever. But I had not taken the time to fully enquire into what the Scriptures truly taught me.

After the conversation between the Lord and Nicodemus, John had recorded Jesus' promise that those who believed in Him would not perish but have eternal life (see John 3:15). Like so many others, I had missed the meaning of the word "eternal." So many people think that believing in Jesus and receiving His salvation is the end of the search. I had believed it was a free pass into heaven. But the words eternal life refer to something quite different from my unthinking assumptions that I had entertained for so many years.

Like our Lord, whatever is eternal has no beginning as well as no end. So how could my life have no beginning? John, who introduced me to the concept of eternal life in his gospel, has the answer to my dilemma. In his first letter he wrote, "And this is the testimony: that God has given us eternal life, and this life is in His Son. He who has the Son [living within] has [eternal] life; he who does not have the Son of God does not have [eternal] life" (1 John 5:11, 12).

The life Jesus bestowed on me when I received His forgiveness is His own life, the life of His Spirit, and it is eternal. That life within me, Jesus' own life, like the life of the Vine and its branches, had no beginning as well as no real end.

Only one question remains. What are the characteristics of the life of the Vine? If I can answer that then I will understand how His life within me is to be expressed. And the Lord Himself provides the answer in His farewell teaching. He gave His disciples three characteristics of His own life. The greatest aspect of His character is expressed in the word we have come to recognize as *agape*, divine love. John's first letter is full of references to that divine love expressed by the Son. Paul describes that same love of our Lord as love that is beyond our capacity to comprehend. It is beyond human knowledge (see Eph. 3:19). This is the pre-eminent characteristics of the life of our Lord flowing through the Vine into its branches and expressed as its fruit (see John 15:9).

The second characteristic of the life of the Vine is found in Jesus' words, "Peace I leave with you, My peace I give to you; not as the world gives do I give to you" (John 14:27). The word translated for "peace" is *eirene*, which refers to "a state of untroubled and undisturbed well-being equivalent with the peace of the Father whose life is eternally without disturbance" (Bullinger, p. 575). Jesus told them that it was His peace, the peace that ruled the life of the Vine and the life of its branches. This peace is beyond human words to explain and describe. It is not human tranquility. This peace, like the Lord's love, has its origin in the courts of heaven itself.

The third characteristic of the life of the Vine is joy. The Lord prayed His joy would remain in the disciples and would fill them (see John 15:11). *Chara* means delight, joy, and gladness. It was described by Peter when he said, "Though now you do not see Him, yet believing, you rejoice with joy inexpressible and full of glory" (1 Peter 1:8). As with His love and His peace, His joy defies human description and human explanation. No one who has been filled with that supreme expression of His eternal life can ever mistake it or seek to replace it with the poverty stricken human substitute. I know it as a song in my heart that sings a love song continually to the Father.

There is one thing that I have left to explore about the Vine. Jesus told the disciples that the purpose of each branch was to bear much fruit. "I am the vine, you are the branches. He who abides in Me, and I in him, bears much fruit; for without Me you can do nothing" (John 15:5). Fruit is the expression of the life of the Vine. No one plants a vineyard and puts up with a vine that has no fruit. We could not possibly expect the Father, who is the Vinedresser, to put up with a branch that is unfruitful. Jesus told them that such branches will be cast out, and they will then wither and burn up.

How then do we understand the fruit that the vine will bear through each of its branches? And for the answer we have to refer again to Paul, who spoke of the fruit of the Spirit, the first three of which are the same love, joy, and peace (see Gal. 5:22). It is a serious mistake to see these fruit as admirable human qualities we can aspire to, just as Jesus' love and joy and peace could never be merely natural human qualities, for they had to flow out of heaven in the life of the Spirit, who makes His dwelling place in each of us.

We are the branches, and the Lord intended that the life of the eternal Spirit flow through each of us bringing forth the same fruit, His love, His joy, and His peace. The Spirit Himself will express those attributes of the character of the Vine in each of us as we fulfill the Lord's instruction, to abide, remain, dwell deeply, and be at rest in Him (see John 15:4–7).

Paul tells us that there are nine fruit of the Spirit (see Gal. 5:22, 23). There are nine ways in which His life and character are expressed. We remind ourselves again that these are not human virtues but the expression of the life of a divine being. He is longsuffering when we transgress. He is kindness and goodness itself. He is faithful and will not deny His own nature. He is the ultimate expression of gentleness, and finally, He is not an arbitrary figure expressing Himself when He pleases; He is the epitome of self-control.

The challenge for each one of us is to live in close company with His Spirit so that we can receive and experience these expressions of His character. Once we have received them, we can learn how to express them in all our dealings with humankind. In that way we will fulfill the purpose He stated in that upper room. This purpose is also His challenge to each of us to love Him and one another in the same way that He has always loved us. This love is the standard for those who are His disciples (see John 13:34, 35).

You Are My Friends

It was a difficult night if you look at it with human eyes. One of His close associates, bidden by Satan, had gone to bring the chief priests and the soldiers to arrest Him for trial and crucifixion. One of those closest to Him would later deny Him, and all the remainder being gripped by fear would desert Him and leave Him to face what lay ahead quite alone. Of all of the men that night, only John would find his way back to the Savior's side in the palace of Annas, the high priest, and there be witness to Peter's denials.

Yet the Lord would not set His love for His disciples to the side, as most of us would when faced with such dire threats as scourging and crucifixion. Because they were closer to Him than all other men, He devoted some of His words that night to comfort, encourage, and instruct them.

In the midst of warning and instructing them, He defined their relationship with Him in a new way. No longer were they to be bond slaves, but they were now His friends because He had entrusted them with all that the Father had told Him (see John 15:14, 15). And in that intimate relationship, He began to reveal what would be in store for them.

As friends He acknowledged their troubled hearts, their fear, and their coming grief by instructing them to not be afraid. In place of their fear, He called them to trust Him and the Father. If they trusted, His peace could rule in their hearts (see John 14:1, 27). And finally He acknowledged what none of them could then foresee, although they may have been dimly aware of it, that they would mourn and weep but that, in spite of what the world believed and said, their tears would turn into rejoicing with time (see John 16:20).

His words could not forestall their coming grief or His prediction that they would all be scattered and would leave Him alone (see John 16:32). But perhaps if they would have gone out of that room dimly knowing that their Lord knew and understood how they felt, their grief would be short lived and on the other side of the terrible chasm of grief would be joy.

Jesus not only spoke of the outcomes of immediate and impending events, but His words took them far out beyond His death, resurrection, and ascension into a world they would explore in the Savior's name (see John 14:29). In that world they would be expelled from the synagogues where they would normally have felt at home. There would be persecution, the world and its inhabitants would hate them, and many would believe that they were doing God a service by killing them (see John 15:18–20; 16:2, 33).

With the predictions of coming distress and persecution, He also foretold work yet to be done in His name, which would be greater than the works He had done. He added that all this would be possible because He would be going to the Father (see John 14:12). And at the heart of their work for Him would be a joint endeavor in which the witness of heaven and their own witness would come together.

When He promised the One who would live in them, walk with them, and go before them to do the Father's will, He began to unfold the enigma. Greater works would be their right because He would send them the One He called the Helper, who would live in them and make greater works possible (see John 15:26, 27). The words "testify" and "bear witness" are translation of the same Greek word *martureo*. This is where we get the word "martyr," which means to bear witness to death. The Spirit's testimony that Jesus was Lord would be at the heart of the disciples' work after Pentecost. And with the Spirit's voice in their inner ears, their own testimony would follow. Jesus had risen from the dead, and they knew their Lord and Savior held out the promise of salvation to all who would believe. But that was still out of reach for those who followed Jesus. The Spirit would soon help them understand these profound mysteries.

The Lord also promised them one further element of their relationship with Him when He told them that whatever they asked in His name the Father would give them and that this was one of the paths to knowing His joy (see John 16:23, 24). Their walk together when they had immediate access to His words and wisdom would not come to an end. Through the Holy One, His own Spirit, who would make His home within each one of His disciples, they could ask the Father in the Lord's name in every situation. No matter how distressing or troublesome their problems were, He would be there with His power available and wisdom ready in whatever situation they faced. Amazingly enough, the same is true for us today.

In His Footsteps

That night I heard the Lord promise us three things that were expressions of His own being: His love, His joy, and His peace. When they left the house that night, and I with them, they would enter a world when all three gifts would be challenged. And from the secure relationship with their Messiah, they would go out into difficulty and horror when fear would grip them, and all would flee.

The Lord's promises would then be severely put to the test, and they would all fail, having only their human abilities to sustain them. The proper fulfillment of His promises of love, joy, and peace would have to wait until the Spirit came. The disciples would find all three gifts fulfilled abundantly in the life where He would live within them. And so it was for me that last day of His human life, as I drank in these promises that were beyond anything I had ever before let into my head and heart.

I knew that day that the challenge to be filled with those expressions of His being crosses time and would forever face me as I embraced my own uncertain future. Perhaps that would be the outcome of the sifting and sorting I would have to pass through. I took on board His promises of peace and love and joy, and I acknowledged that the human abilities I was born with were not up to the task.

I knew well how to dwell in the world. Its surroundings, attitudes, and desires were very familiar to me, and I found myself reluctant to admit that the world had left its imprint on my soul. I knew that imprint would have to be dealt with and erased. I acknowledged that afternoon that I did not know how to abide, dwell securely, and be at home in Him, despite the doctrine being familiar.

As I faced into the last hours of His and my walk to Golgotha, I embraced those challenges and looked for His Spirit's instruction to teach me how to abide in my Lord and Master, who was about to die. And then I had a thought: if I wanted to abide in His life, would that mean that I had to abide in His death as well?

Chapter Eleven
THURSDAY NIGHT: The Hour Has Come

The Lord's Prayer

That Thursday night the Lord began the last part of His walk to Golgotha. He went out of the city, across the Kidron Valley, and into the quiet of Gethsemane. But before He left the house with His disciples and probably in the company of John, He prayed with words that reveal so much of our Lord's relationship with His Father, with His disciples, and with the world of believers, who would one day become part of His kingdom.

It is hardly likely that He would have spoken these final words to His Father as He walked through and out of the city or when they entered the garden. Somewhere that evening, and before He came to Gethsemane, our Lord turned away from His disciples and faced towards heaven for what should properly be called the Lord's prayer.

There are few words in the Scriptures that have the power as these do to take us deep into the heart of the Son's relationship with His Father. Some would look for doctrine in this prayer, but that is a profound mistake. The Lord's words enshrine what He considered most important for Himself, for His disciples, and for those whom would one day believe on His name.

His words contain kernels of truth that may, when properly examined, blossom into principles, which will govern the lives of all who follow Him, myself included. And it is in that attitude that I begin this examination into this expression of the relationship between eternal Father and eternal Son.

Glorify Your Son

The Lord began His prayer with an admission to the Father, who had directed each step of His walk to Golgotha. "Father, the hour has come. Glorify Your Son, that Your Son also may glorify You" (John 17:1). The word translated for "glorify" is *doxazo,* and this part of His prayer is a cry for the Father to invest Him with dignity, make Him important in His Father's eyes, and place Him in an honorable position before His Father. This was in sharp contrast to what Satan and the Jewish leaders had planned for Him. Crucifixion was not an honorable death. It was an expression to the unfeeling populace of shame and degradation. There was no dignity or glory for the Lord hanging there between two thieves.

His eyes were on the Father because He had directed His Son to that moment. The glory that was the subject of His prayer referred to the honor and dignity He desired to receive from the heart of the Father, not from those who jeered Him on the cross.

The Lord's prayer that He would share the Father's glory is one aspect of their relationship, but there were other parts of His glory for us to consider. The glory He was seeking from the Father, He had previously known before the world began (see John 17:5). This idea was at terrible odds with the fate that so inexorably waited for Him on the cross. And it is here where you and I become part of the story. Giving up the glory He shared with the Father in the most intimate of relationships before the world began was part of the cost of our salvation.

To make this salvation happen, He also had to receive something else from the Father. He spoke of it in His prayer. "You have given Him [the Son of Man] authority over all flesh, that He should give eternal life to as many as You have given Him" (John 17:2). The more I read of my Lord, the more I am confounded and in awe of Him. In my self-centeredness, I had so often thought that my salvation came about because I had made a choice so long ago. Even though my choice is certainly part of the equation, Jesus already knew thousands of years ago that I could only become a child of the Father because the Father had mysteriously given me to my Lord. In that special sense, I was a gift to the Son so that He could be the eldest Son in the growing family of God (see Rom. 8:29).

That was part of the work He came to do when He affirmed, "I have finished [literally: am finishing] the work which You have given Me to do" (John 17:4), which involved buying the world's salvation, which included purchasing the gift of me and so many uncountable others. I doubt that I will fully understood that truth this side of heaven, but I bury it in my mind and heart so that a little more of this truth may be added to my comprehension each year as I draw closer to Him.

The Men You Have Given Me

The Lord's prayer for His eleven disciples follows. They were on His heart as He neared Golgotha as well as all those who followed Him, including us who live in this present age. Four things were true of those disciples and potentially true of us.

Jesus affirmed to the Father that His disciples had kept the Father's word, which was revealed to them in the Person of the Living Word (see John 1:1; Rev. 19:13). The word "kept" is from the verb *tereo*, and it refers to each disciples making an initial choice "to watch over, to take care of, to keep an eye on, to observe attentively the living Word, Jesus of Nazareth, who had come and made His dwelling place in each of them." That was a choice that continued throughout their lifetime. Jesus, the Living Word, was the subject of the lives of those first disciples, and there was no other focus for them, and they would never have another focus as long as they remained true to their calling.

Jesus spoke again of His disciples when He told the Father that he had given His disciples all the words He had received from the Father (see John 17:8). In these words, the Lord subtly changes the subject though the change is not apparent in English. Jesus did not use the broader term *logos* referring to Himself and to all that He speaks into the world. He replaced it with the word *rhema*, which has a more restricted meaning and refers to "something which, at a particular point of time is spoken, a sentence, a saying, a speech, a declaration, a command, or a promise" (Bullinger, p. 897).

The Father initially spoke His separate words, His *rhema,* to the Lord Jesus, who spoke each word to the disciples. And the compliment our Lord pays the disciples is that they received each *rhema* He delivered to them. The word "received" affirms that they did not receive each word like a letter dropped into the mailbox. Instead, they took hold of each word, apprehended it, and made it a living part of their lives.

We have the advantage of understanding the separate words the Father spoke to Jesus and that He in turn spoke to His disciples, for the Gospels contain that sacred record. But there is a trap here. Reading, understanding, and committing each word to memory as good doctrine does not fit the Lord's compliment about His disciples receiving each spoken word. During the Lord's walk with His disciples, the Holy Spirit invested each word the Lord Jesus spoke to them with the meanings the Father intended. His disciples then received, apprehended, and applied each word in their lives. There was no static doctrine here, only living practice. And the same applies to all His disciples across the ages, who desire to fulfill their calling as sons and daughters of the living God.

The third aspect of the lives of His disciples is found in the Lord's affirmation that His disciples did not belong in the world and that their lives were not patterned after the principles of the world. He had shown them the way for He also was not part of this world (see John 17:16). The world where our Lord lived was an alien place, completely different from the world of His Spirit, which was His eternal dwelling place. He was not born of the world, for His birth involved an action of the Holy Spirit in the womb of Mary.

The lives for the first disciples were closely patterned on the Lord's life. He was not of the world and neither were they. After Pentecost they would owe their birth in the family of the Father to an action of the Father's Spirit. And it would be from that same Spirit that the power would come for them to carry out the Lord's command to go into all the world and proclaim the good news of His salvation (see Acts 1:5, 8).

The final parallel between the lives of the first disciples, who were also not of this world, and His disciples in this day brings us face to face with our sometimes desperate need for approval. Jesus had His approval from the Father on a number of occasions (see Matt. 3:17; 17:5), and Paul wrote of the same principle in his letter to the church in Galatia, "For do I now persuade men, or God? Or do I seek to please men? For if I still pleased men, I would not be a bond servant of Christ" (Gal. 1:10). Embedded in his declaration is the teaching that it is from the Lord, and not from humankind, that we should seek approval in all that we do. This is a challenge that followers of Christ have faced across the centuries.

The fourth observation the Lord made about His disciples was framed in His assertion to the Father that He had sent them into the world and for that reason had sanctified them, set them apart, for this service in the same way that He had been set apart for the service committed to Him by the Father (see John 17:18, 19).

The world for those disciples and for us is a dangerous place. Among those opposed to the gospel—and there are so many—opposition may take the form of words, and in extreme cases, opposition takes the form of persecution leading to death. And this has always been the case around the world where the gospel has exposed the sterile artificiality of life in the world and, unhappily, exposed the aridity of established religions.

But there is another danger in the world for those who follow our Lord. Paul described the principles of the world as weak and beggarly (see Gal. 4:9). He was referring to the principles that undergird all the life, operations, and works of the world. Like beggars, these principles have no power. They ask for everything, but they give nothing. They provoke desire, but when desire is supposedly satisfied, it remains intact and lives on to continually plague the disciple for another day.

We are surrounded by these world principles all day, every day. The noises of futility claim our attention, seeking to arouse desire which, though we follow where it leads, can never be satisfied. And the world also panders to our lust for outrageous and titillating information: murder, disaster, another weeping interviewee, and countless obscenities of figure, action, and dress. And the more we let these principles and works of the world find a home in our attention, the more we are pleasing the world and the rulers of this world.

John put our choice abruptly using a word the Lord used as the central element in our relationship with the Father. Love. Agape. John issued an instruction and a warning to the disciples to whom this letter was addressed. They were not to prostitute the love, agape, they had received from the Father and focus it on the things of the world. If they did, the love of the Father would be withdrawn (see 1 John 2:15). Like John's readers, every disciple and would-be disciple around the world has the ability to prostitute the divine love the Spirit pours into our hearts by making the world, and not the Lord God and each other, the object of that love.

In place of the Father's intended objects for His love, Him and each other, the patterns of the old nature surface, and we direct our admiration, respect, and reverence to elements of the world that the Lord despises. And in so doing, we focus our service away from the Lord and His people and give our obedience to those same weak and beggarly elements of the world. Paul echoed this truth when he told the disciples in the church at Rome that they would become slaves of sin and of their sinful nature if they yielded their obedience to sin and to that evil nature. On the other hand, if they yielded themselves to God, they would become His servants (see Rom. 6:16). And the apostle might have added: it's entirely your choice!

But there was another part of the Lord's prayer that puts a formidable barrier between the disciple and all the manifold dangers of the world. Jesus told them, "And for their sakes I sanctify Myself, that they also may be sanctified by the truth" (John 17:19).

Jesus was set apart for a future life of service leading to Golgotha when He was baptized by John in the River Jordan. This is what the term "sanctify" means. At that time He, in effect, died to the old life and was sanctified for the service that lay in front of Him, by the Father through the Spirit, who descended on Him like a dove.

His disciples believed that to be sanctified means to be set part from the world and from the life of self-pleasing. In that way the focus of their lives changed from their focus on self and on the world to the right focus on the Lord Himself. And so they were equipped to go into all the world and proclaim the gospel of our Lord.

For us in this day, we also have the choice to ask the Lord to set our willing hearts and minds apart for His love and service. Being set apart changes the way we look at things. Being sanctified to the Lord's service gives us a mindset that helps us resist all the blandishments of the world, which seek to draw us away from obedience and love for our Lord and back into the sticky snares of our adversary.

That They May Be One

The Lord's final focus in that most private prayer to the Father was "for those who will believe in Me through their word" (John 17:20). He had shifted His gaze from the immediate disciples to those who through all time would make the choice to follow Him. And His prayer has a deliberate and alarming focus. The Lord set a standard that has so often been ignored in Christian circles. He prayed that all His disciples, both those who had met with Him in the upper room and all those who would later follow Him, would be one in the same way that He and the Father are one (see John 17:21).

The word Jesus used and is translated as "one" is emphatic, referring to His purpose that all disciples everywhere, through all time, would emphatically be one single entity, one body, one church. Some have interpreted Jesus' words as referring to inner unity of the heart, but behind the tragedy of so many denominations and independent churches (at last count, more than 33,000 of them), there are passionate advocates of this or that church with the sometimes unspoken inference that others have missed the boat and are adrift in a wilderness of mistaken doctrine or practice or pattern of government. Nothing of heart unity could exist in such attitudes, and I wonder at the Lord's views of such formidable disunity when He prayed that they all may be one.

The oneness of Father and Son is the pattern, not the earthly pattern of human organizations but the divine pattern established in the kingdom of heaven. Nothing can ever disturb the sacred oneness the Lord referred to. In that fellowship the sharing of their lives at the deepest level was because of love. You can see love in the Father, who is the definition of love, the Son, who through His life expressed that love in the world, and the Spirit, who continually pours the Father's love into the hearts of those who truly believe.

When we apply that divine pattern to the lives of today's disciples, we have to face the supreme challenge of understanding what divides one from the other. We then have to lay it aside as a sacrifice to the Father, pray that others will come to the same mind, and let His love for each other overflow in our hearts. For in so doing, we will fulfill the Lord's words to the Father "that they may be one just as We are one: I in them, and You in Me; that they may be made perfect [complete] in one, and that the world may know that You have sent Me, and have loved them as You have loved Me" (John 17:22, 23).

What does divide us? What obstacles have the world, the flesh, and the devil put in the way of that oneness of love? The list is so long that it would overflow this page and more. But mature reflection with the Spirit taking part in our thinking will make clear what divides me from you. My brother whom I meet every day has the power to enrich me and I him, and I must not put any obstacles in the way of that transaction.

I Have Known You

Our Lord concluded His prayer to the Father with His own reflection on that relationship and on what had been achieved. "O righteous Father! The world has not known You, but I have known You" (John 17:25). Everything hinges on that knowing. His disciples knew that the Father had sent Him, knew that He declared to them the name of the Father, and they knew that the Father's love had become enshrined in the Son. The final part of His prayer is His affirmation, "And I have declared to them Your name, and will declare it, that the love with which You loved Me may be in them, and I in them" (John 17:26).

The Father's love was His ultimate gift to His disciples and is beyond anything this world could devise. Nothing in religion comes close to that love and the One through whom love is expressed. And I take to heart the Lord's words: the love of the Father with the Lord Himself may dwell in the inner shrine of my heart, and there it will fill up every corner and crevice of my being.

This is what I take from this prayer of the Son to the Father. This application was truly spoken that night and is spoken again by the same Spirit into my own heart. To be filled to the fullness of my being with the Creator of all things, Jesus of Nazareth, the One who is light and love and wisdom is a gift beyond price. Nothing in heaven or on earth comes close to that incomparable gift.

Agony

As Judas was fetching the Jewish leaders and the squad of Roman soldiers, Jesus was in Gethsemane facing a revelation from the Father that profoundly disturbed Him. We make this assumption because of what we know about the Son of the Father as recorded in the four Gospels. Jesus left eight of His disciples near the garden's entrance and only taking Peter, James, and John, He withdrew into the quiet depths of the olive grove. There He addressed the Father in the most heartfelt prayer of His life.

Mark records that Jesus "began to be troubled and deeply distressed" (Mark 14:33). The words that Mark used tell us that something profound happened to the Lord. The word "began" is a Greek verb that speaks of something that occurred at a point in time and had profound continuing consequences. With the delicacy of one who loved his Lord, Mark does not tell us what came into existence at that moment, only that Jesus was troubled and deeply distressed. If we are going to look, with tender and a humble reluctance, into the mind and heart of our Lord, we need to attend to two other key words in our inquiry into what happened between the Father and the Son that night.

I have learned that the translations of two Greek words Jesus used cannot do justice to their true meanings. These two Greek words translated "troubled" and "deeply distressed" depict the greatest possible degree of infinite horror and suffering, suggestive of shuddering awe and fear.

I cannot possibly come close to the horror Christ must have been facing. If He were to drink the cup and save the world, He had to take not only my own sins and the sins of those I love on His shoulders, but also the sins of every man, woman, and child living at any time on the planet. Hitler and the sins of the Holocaust were included. Massacres in Cambodia, every murder, torture, rape, extortion, deceit, and every evil, shameful event on the face of the earth were included in that catalogue. By agreeing to be the sacrificial Lamb, all those sins—the list is endless—would be embedded in the heart and soul of the One who knew no sin and whose love for you and me took Him to Golgotha.

Jesus knew there was no escape from His inner turmoil of grief. It would be the environment in which He spent His last hours. He then told His disciples to stay where they were and keep watch while He went into the depths of the garden. There He turned His face to the Father and prayed: "Abba, Father, all things are possible for You. Take this cup away from Me; nevertheless, not what I will, but what You will" (Mark 14:36).

After this prayer Jesus checked on His three disciples, and finding them asleep, urged them to join Him in prayer before returning to talk to His Father once again. But this time during His prayer there is a small compelling difference. "O My Father, if this cup cannot pass away from Me unless I drink it, Your will be done" (Matt. 26:42). In His first prayer, He acknowledged that the cup of infinite horror existed. In His second prayer, He accepted that if the Father willed it, He would drink it. This was also the subject of His third prayer.

Luke adds two postscripts that add verity to the record, He records that after His second prayer an angel from heaven, obviously sent by the Father, appeared to Jesus and strengthened Him (see Luke 22:43). The Father had a great compassion for the One who would suffer on behalf of all of us. So an angel was sent to the Savior's side in the Garden of Gethsemane to strengthen Him, for His suffering could not wait until Golgotha. It had already begun.

Luke's second postscript reveals that in the Savior's agony He prayed more earnestly to the Father and that His sweat became like great drops of blood (see Luke 22:44). It was not only His inner soul that suffered. The word translated "agony" refers to "bodily strife, struggle, violent struggle, or agony, both of body and mind" (Bullinger, p. 36). And one outcome of the shuddering horror that wracked Him appeared in His body as sweat like great drops of blood falling to the ground.

Then it was over. He understood that He could not escape the physical or mental pain, but the contemplation of the cup He must drink was interrupted by the temporary release of immediate concerns. Judas was approaching with the soldiers, and the Lord's footsteps to Golgotha were quickly decreasing in number.

In His Footsteps

I had faced the knowledge of my Lord's crucifixion and found it terribly hard to handle. The knowledge of what it would cost Him to bear all the sins of humankind in His own body was beyond me. I could see it. My mind could begin to understand it, but my understanding of the cost of that cup was limited by the limitations of my own mind.

It was as though I had begun the long walk from Jericho to Golgotha in some kind of innocent ignorance, but I now found myself confronted by a darkness so vile and deep that my soul shrank from contemplating it. I was glad that the disciples were asleep.

I found myself becoming angry at the thoughtlessness of so many who abuse the Lord's cry about the cup and turn it into some kind of prosaic artifact of life and religion. No one could ever and would ever be able to comprehend the horrors that filled that cup. He would drain that cup it to its terrible depths.

The knowledge of what He would suffer in His pure and beautiful Spirit would be forever part of the gift He gives me. And I have to accept that the glory of His gift of life and salvation is forever to be mixed with the knowledge of what it meant for Him to suffer for the sins of the world, mine included.

That night I had to accept that I cannot divorce the wonder of my salvation and the continuing gift of His grace from the terrible cost of that cup, when He would drink to the full all the unspeakable horrors of the sins of humankind. Then Judas came, and my Lord's final footsteps to Golgotha had begun.

Chapter Twelve
THURSDAY NIGHT and FRIDAY MORNING: They All Forsook Him

Whoever I Kiss

They stood together at the entrance of the Garden of Gethsemane, and a group made up of Jewish leaders, soldiers, angry civilians, and Judas crowded around the Lord and His disciples. Most of us know that the sign of Judas' betrayal was a kiss and that Jesus then asked the betrayer, whom He called friend, why he had come (see Matt. 26:50). Friend! This term Jesus used here was not for someone who had an intimate relationship with Him. The Lord would not dignify His relationship with Judas beyond the truth. Instead, He used a word that could be translated into "companion, associate, or comrade" (Bullinger, p. 308), not intimate friend, beloved, or one held most dear. And yet, even in that last encounter, the Lord, being true to His nature, was reaching out to His betrayer.

The reactions of those around Him that night reveal the turmoil that had descended among them. Peter took out his sword and struck off the ear of the servant of the high priest. The Jewish leaders were triumphant at last, and the crowd of civilians, unlike those who followed Him waving palm branches, were caught up in some kind of mass hysteria. The disciples were trapped in fear when they bound the Lord and led Him away. This fear immobilized their devotion to their Lord, and they all left Him; nine went into the darkness of Jerusalem, and two, Peter and John, trailed along in their Lord's footsteps.

This division of men into two groups, those who wanted Him dead and those who followed Him, fulfilled Jesus' words earlier in His ministry, "Do not think that I came to bring peace on earth. I did not come to bring peace but a sword" (Matt. 10:34). It is true that He came to call all people unto Himself (see John 12:32), but the living truth that He expressed among men and women would not only heal divisions but also cause them. For so many then and today, the Lord's call to follow Him will not be received. It will be, in some cases, bitterly resisted and often expressed in persecution.

What followed that night is found in records that have two strands. The first is the record of what happened to our Lord before He began the final part of His journey to Golgotha. The second strand in the story reveals the reactions of the men and women who were bound into those final events. Records of the five trials that followed are spread over the four gospels, and we have to rely on a harmony of the gospels for our understanding of the sequence of events.

Five Trials and a Scourging

The soldiers first took Jesus to Annas, who was a senior man in the hierarchy of priests. According to contemporary records, he was enormously wealthy from the temple trade and was politically unscrupulous. Annas was also the father-in-law of Caiaphas, who was the high priest that year. There the squad of Roman soldiers was dismissed.

The conversation between Jesus and Annas was brief. Annas asked Jesus about His teaching and His disciples, but there was no anger in his words such as would later spill over when Jesus stood before the Sanhedrin. Jesus replied that He had been teaching publically and that many had heard His words. He told Annas to ask those who had heard Him speak in public, for they knew what he had said (see John 18:21). And although one of those present struck the Lord, there was no other evidence of that anger. Annas sent Him bound to Caiaphas.

Very early that Friday morning, while it was yet dark, Jesus was delivered by the servants of the high priests and of the Sanhedrin into the courtyard of Caiaphas' house where Peter would later deny His Lord. There the soldiers mocked and beat Him. They blindfolded Him and struck Him on the face, demanding that He prophesy, and when He said nothing, they spoke to Him irreverently (see Luke 22:64, 65). But these were small indignities compared to what was to follow.

From the courtyard they took our Lord up the flight of courtyard stairs into the council chamber where the elders of the people, the chief priests, and scribes had gathered for an impromptu meeting of the ruling Jewish council. We have to wonder from the silence of the sacred record about whether Joseph of Arimathea and Nicodemus were present and how they would have responded to seeing Jesus treated in such a way.

According to the rules of the Sanhedrin, there had to be proven testimony from two or three witnesses before a verdict of death could be imposed. The only way the chief priests, elders, and members of the council could be sure of putting Him to death was through the use of false witnesses (see Matt. 26:59, 60). But their hate for the Lord overrode all the legal requirements of the Sanhedrin, so they found two false witnesses who testified that two years previously Jesus had told the people that if they destroyed the temple He would restore it within three days (see John 2:19).

But their testimony, which was accurate enough, was not the source of Caiaphas' anger. Turning from the false witnesses to Jesus, the high priest said, "I put You under oath by the living God: Tell us if You are the Christ, the Son of God!" (Matt. 26:63). At that point Jesus broke His silence. How could He not, even though His response would certainly result in His condemnation to death? In the ears of those who interrogated Him, He would most certainly be accused of blasphemy, so He answered, "It is as you said. Nevertheless, I say to you, hereafter you will see the Son of Man sitting at the right hand of the Power [of God], and coming on the clouds of heaven" (Matt. 26:64).

Our Lord had been instrumental in words and actions that would bring about His own crucifixion two different times in His life. He had chosen Judas, knowing that a demon lived within him. And here His own words, spoken under oath, would most certainly lead to His condemnation to death for blasphemy. And it was so. "'What do you think?' [the high priest asked]. They answered and said, 'He is deserving of death'" (Matt. 26:66).

Now the Sanhedrin had a problem. They only had religious power. The civil power to condemn a person to death lay in the hands of the Roman authorities. This meant that they had to go to Pontius Pilate.

The governor's palace was only a short distance from the palace of the high priest, and the servants of the high priests delivered our Lord there in the very early hours of the morning. We don't know if the governor was awake at that early hour, probably not, but he had a retinue of servants who would have woken him with the news that the one who called Himself the Christ had been brought by the Sanhedrin. Taking his place on the judgment seat, Pilate asked Jesus if He was the King of the Jews, and Jesus affirmed that He was (see Matt. 27:11).

That was not enough for the leaders of the Jews, who also stood before the judgment seat. They began to accuse Him, but Jesus remained silent. Even Pilate was impressed, so He added his voice to theirs. But Jesus still remained silent, fulfilling the ancient prophecy, "He was oppressed and He was afflicted, yet He opened not His mouth; He was led as a lamb to the slaughter, and as a sheep before its shearers is silent, so He opened not His mouth" (Isa. 53:7).

Pilate told the chief priests that he found no fault in Jesus, but this response only drew greater anger from the Jewish leaders who added the accusation that through

His teaching the Lord stirred up the people all the way from Galilee to Jerusalem (see Luke 23:5). Pilate then asked whether Jesus was a Galilean and when finding that it was so, he saw a way out of his responsibilities and sent Jesus to Herod Antipas who, as procurator under the Romans, had jurisdiction over Galilee.

Pilate's way out was short-lived. Herod wasn't interested in the political and legal aspects of the case, but having heard through the grapevine of Jesus' miracles, Herod hoped to see something that would titillate his unintelligent and spurious interest. And of course he was disappointed, for Jesus said nothing and did nothing. So Herod and his men of war treated the Lord with contempt. They mocked and derided Him, and after they dressed Him in a purple robe, they sent Him back to Pilate.

Now, finally, the last act of this eternal drama begins to play out its tragedy. We may leave out the detail that only bears us along to the inevitable and terrible end and focus on three related acts. Pilate had received Jesus back at his palace and taking his place again on the judgment seat, he received word from his wife that she had suffered greatly because of a dream and that he should have nothing to do with this just man (see Matt. 27:19).

We are faced with a puzzling situation. Why should the Lord God intrude into the dreams of this Gentile woman with a dream that could make no difference to the outcome? Sitting on his judgment seat, Pilate obviously heard the message, but he apparently took no notice. So the answer to our puzzle has to wait until all things are revealed to the children of the Most High in some distant administration of the kingdom.

The second related act involves another puzzle. It was the custom in political circles for the governor to release one criminal as a mark of his respect for the Jewish religion at the Passover feast. And at that time, while Jesus was standing tethered to his guards, the criminal Barabbas was included in the narrative. Pilate addressed the Satan-following crowd and said to them, "'Which of the two do you want me to release to you?' They said, 'Barabbas!' Pilate said to them, 'What then shall I do with Jesus who is called Christ?' They all said to him, 'Let Him be crucified!'" (Matt. 27:21, 22).

The irony is that the name of this feared criminal was Barabbas, which literally means "son of the father." So the choice had to be made by the crowd to either release this "son of the father" or crucify the true Son of the Father. Even Pilate's attempt at appeasing the crowd with the question, "Why, what evil has He done?" drew no response other that the irrational cry of the tumult bound on His destruction. Pilate then washed his hands in front of the angry crowd and told them that he was innocent of the blood of Jesus, for he had found him guiltless of any crime. As if the washing of his hands could absolve the governor from his part in the looming crucifixion.

The cry of the mob, "His blood be on us and on our children" soon found its just fulfillment. Barely forty years were to pass before Jerusalem would be surrounded by the ring of crosses holding up to the heavens the testimony that His blood was being held to their account.

The third act in the drama then unfolded. Jesus was bound to a stake outside the Praetorium, stripped of His clothes, and mercilessly beaten with a whip of many cords laced with bone and iron that tore great gashes into His face and body so that, as the prophet wrote, "His visage was marred more than any man, and His form more than the sons of men" (Isa. 52:14). And all this, for our transgressions.

Can any of us stand idly by and give our assent without flinching to that terrible prophecy, "He was bruised for our iniquities; the chastisement for our peace was upon Him, and by His stripes we are healed" (Isa. 53:5). Can we stand and watch the final mockery of His royal being as they stripped Him, gowned Him with a scarlet robe, wove a crown of thorns and pressed it down so that His blood again poured out?

And there in the Praetorium, the Roman soldiers mocked Him with a rod for a scepter and bowed before Him and called him King of the Jews (see Matt. 27:29). Having said that, they took the reed away, struck Him with it, took off the blasphemous robe of kingship, clothed Him in His own clothes, and led Him away to be crucified.

The Thirty Pieces of Silver

There was another death that day, and one that cast an unhappy light on the one who could least afford it. Judas must have been watching when Pilate delivered his verdict to take the Lord away and crucify Him. Something stirred in his heart. Matthew reports that Judas, knowing the outcome of His betrayal, was remorseful. The Greek word does not refer to the remorse that leads to true repentance, but instead to the act of becoming dissatisfied and anxious with what has happened, and as a result, a change is made in the purpose but not in the heart.

Judas took the thirty pieces of silver, went to the temple, and threw them at the feet of those present. The anguish of his soul is etched into his words to the chief priests and elders, "I have sinned by betraying innocent blood." And on the reverse side of the coin, the priests' hardness of heart is also etched into their reply. "What is that to us? You see to it!" (Matt. 27:4).

Looking on from the twenty-first century, one could hope that there truly had been a change in the heart of this one whom Jesus also loved. Judas had been with

Jesus for nearly three years and surely would have heard His words foretelling His crucifixion. Did his words, "I have betrayed innocent blood" amount to self-deception? And could there be redemption for Judas bought and paid for on the cross as there is for all of us? We don't know. All we have are Jesus' words that the Son of man would indeed go to His death as it had been prophesied but woe to the man who would betray Him (see Matt. 26:24). The eternal destiny of Judas has mercifully been hidden from our eyes view, and speculation is pointless.

Matthew reports that Judas went out and hanged himself. The details are missing, but from other authorities we can assume his likely progress from the city. Probably after He crossed the Valley of Hinnom, he climbed the steep slopes of the mountain on the valley's far side. There he unwound his girdle, tied it around his neck, and onto the branch of a nearby tree. He leapt out over the jagged rocks of the valley side. The branch broke under his weight, and he fell onto the rocks, where still alive, though probably unconscious, his stomach ruptured and he died (see Acts 1:18).

The Disciple Whom Jesus Loved

The second person we encounter in this record of the Lord's trials and scourging is John, the beloved disciple. When his Lord was bound and led away to see Annas, Matthew reports that all the disciples forsook Him and fled (see Matt. 26:56; Mark 14:50). John reports that Peter followed Jesus from a distance and that he, who was known by the high priest, entered the courtyard with Jesus (see John 18:15).

We believe that John was a man of some note and reputation in Jerusalem. It is likely that he or his family owned the house that Nicodemus had come to so early in the Lord's ministry, and it is also likely that this house was the residence where John took Jesus' mother as Jesus hung dying on the cross (we will deal with that account in our next chapter).

John went into the house of Caiaphas while Peter remained outside. John would then have been present in the courtyard of that house when Jesus was led bound up the stairs to the large council chamber on the second floor. And it is likely, though there are no records to confirm this assumption, that the beloved disciple was present among those who also followed the Lord from trial to trial and to His final conviction. He was not there as a participant in their rage, but as one whose heart was deeply grieved by what his Lord was suffering.

It is most likely that John stood outside the Praetorium where Jesus was lashed to the stake and then flogged. We can only imagine John's pain as he saw the flesh stripped from his beloved Lord's body.

We next encounter John at the cross, and we can safely assume that his heart was filled with indescribable grief as he walked among the crowd along what is now called the *Via Dolorosa* (Way of Grief), watching every stumbling step of his Savior's last footsteps to Golgotha.

Peter Followed at a Distance

Luke reports that Peter followed Jesus at a distance, keeping his Lord in sight but staying far enough away so that he would not draw attention to himself. John also must have been following the Lord for somehow Peter and John were together at the entrance to the high priest's palace. Their paths are unknown to us as are any words they may have said to each other about what was happening to their Lord. And when they came to the palace of Caiaphas, Peter remained outside until John spoke with the servant doorkeeper. Peter was then admitted to the courtyard where he would deny that he knew Jesus.

The story of Peter's denials began in the upper room. Matthew, Mark, and Luke report what the Lord said to His disciples, especially Peter. The reports in Matthew and Mark are virtually identical with Luke adding significant details that fill out the record and provide additional insights into both the Lord's view of His errant disciple and Peter's earnest commitment to his Lord.

After the Lord had instituted the Lord's Supper, He turned to Peter and said, "All of you will be made to stumble because of Me this night, for it is written: 'I will strike the Shepherd, and the sheep of the flock will be scattered'" (Matt. 26:31). Peter replied with his characteristic and unthinking bravado, "Even if all are made to stumble because of You, I will never be made to stumble" (Matt. 26:33).

We remember that the name the Lord gave Peter was *petros*, a stone held in the hand, or rolled along the ground or even thrown away. The Lord did not invest stability in that name. We turn to Luke's report of the Lord's reply. "Simon, Simon! Indeed, Satan has asked for you, that he may sift you as wheat" (Luke 22:31).

The shaking that Satan asked for certainly took place. Peter was shaken between extremes like wheat on a sieve. He protested that he would never stumble and that he would follow the Lord and die with Him. But in actuality, Satan asked that he tempt Peter to follow at a distance out of fear that he would be caught up and be crucified like his Lord. And in this short time, Satan planned to create so much distance between Peter and his Lord that he would finally deny that he ever knew Him. Satan's request had indeed been heard in the councils of heaven

But there was another request before the Father at that time, as there always will be when His children are in dire straits from the enemy's attacks. We hold firm to the Lord's promise that He will be near us, not that we will be spared the trial, but that our faith in our glorious Lord will grow and not fail (see Luke 22:32). It is important to note that the Lord did not pray that Peter would be spared the turmoil and distress of his denials and of the grief that would follow.

The purpose of sieving the wheat was to separate the good grain from the chaff. Let the chaff be blown away for the good grain to be retained. And this was the agenda of the Lord's prayer for Peter. The real grain that would be left when the sieving was over was the faith that the Lord prayed would not fail. He needed His errant disciple to "strengthen his brethren," who had also fled into the night, perhaps pursued by the same terrible demons of doubt, fear, and anxiety.

The dialogue between Jesus and Peter continued. He told the Lord with the earnest commitment that was true to his character as *petros*, the stone which could be thrown away and discarded, that he was ready to go to prison and die for the Lord. The Lord replied that the rooster would crow after Peter had denied his Lord three times (see Luke 22:33, 34).

The images of Peter in the courtyard of Caiaphas' palace are compelling. We find him sitting with the servants around the fire that someone had lit and then, when asked, spoke in words that would come back to haunt him. His accent was Galilean and easily recognized among the people in the courtyard, who would all have most likely been Judean. And so his own voice betrayed himself to his listeners.

At that time the Lord was upstairs in the council chamber at trial before the Sanhedrin, but when it was over He was led out onto the balcony on the way to the palace of Pilate. Peter would have looked up and seen his Lord, bound and being led away. At that time Jesus looked down from the upper balcony and their eyes met. Luke reports that the Lord turned and looked at Peter (see Luke 22:61). The Spirit draws a veil over what was contained in the Lord's gaze and over Peter's first thoughts. What we are left with are different reports of the four gospel writers. The one quoted here is from Luke, who wrote that Peter remembered the word of the Lord and His prediction about denying the Lord. The memory filled the errant disciple with the deepest grief (see Luke 22:61, 62). The Greek words Luke used tell us that Peter's tears were painful and cruel.

At that point Peter's part in the Lord's footsteps to Golgotha came to an abrupt end. Like Judas, he went out into the night, but unlike the betrayer, redemption would certainly follow.

In His Footsteps

During the long walk to Golgotha, I had encountered many choices and one of them confronted me that night. Did I follow Him at a distance like Peter, afraid that my association with Him would imperil my life and future or, at the very least, put my relationships with others at risk? Or was I like John, able to enter the place of His judgment and there associate myself with the imperiled One?

That night the choice was there, and I stumbled over it. On the one hand, the pleadings of my old nature told me that I should stop walking in His footsteps in case I should, like Him, be condemned. On the other hand, I had accepted the invitation to follow the One I acknowledged as Creator of all things and Lord of my life wherever He was to go. And so I hesitated.

Then I saw Him looking at Peter from the upper balcony with eyes full of compassion and utterly devoid of judgment. In that moment I embraced the certainty of His forgiveness for my hesitancy, and the choice was made. I would follow Him the rest of the way to Golgotha.

I knew that I had yet to understand and embrace the principles that underlay His invitation to take up my cross and follow Him. So I stood with the others, opponents and followers alike, at the cross and sought the inner illumination that would fill up my understanding of all that was to take place that last day of His earthly life. Only then would I be equipped to do what He commanded. His cross, and therefore my cross, still lay ahead. It was there for me to embrace, if I had the courage and the commitment to embrace it.

Chapter Thirteen
FRIDAY: The Cross

Introduction

I have followed Him in mind and spirit from the ancient city of Jericho near the Jordan, up into the Judean hills, and to the city that bears His name, and I have now come to the final part of my journey. I must follow Him through the last days of the human life the Father decreed for His Son. That journey is nearly at an end, for the last footsteps will take Him to the Place of a Skull where my Lord will be crucified.

My journey is not at an end; it is more likely turned into a new beginning. I am aware that I do not follow the Lord to Golgotha alone, for a number of others, both men and women, completed that journey nearly two millennia ago.

As I walk these last steps into history, I look out for those who also walk this way. I hope to find in their lives some images, however fragmentary and incomplete, of my own inner journey. And finding those images and allowing Him to imprint the truth of those images on my own inner man, my search will take my next upward steps on the long climb to being conformed to the image of His Son (see Rom. 8:29). And if He gives me grace for this journey, it will be because He also has His eyes on me, as He had His eyes on Peter in the palace of Caiaphas. Through His grace I will discover more of what it means to take up my own cross, follow Him, and be His disciple.

Part One: And They Crucified Him

The Praetorium

"So [Pilate] ... delivered Jesus, after he had scourged Him, to be crucified. Then the soldiers led Him away into the hall called Praetorium, and they called together the whole garrison. And they clothed Him with purple; and they twisted a crown of thorns, put it on His head, and began to salute Him, 'Hail, King of the Jews!' Then they struck Him on the head with a reed and spat on Him; and bowing the knee, they worshiped Him. And when they had mocked Him, they took the purple off Him, put His own clothes on Him, and led Him out to crucify Him" (Mark 15:15–20).

There was another man with the Lord that early morning. Like me, He was a Gentile, but unlike me, he was a centurion in charge of a cohort of soldiers. These soldiers were the ones who, at his orders, stripped the Lord and tied Him to the stake in preparation for the scourging that Pilate had ordered. When the Son of Man was taken down from that bloody stake, the centurion would have ordered his men to bring out the cross, the nails, the hammer, and the script that would be fastened above the Savior's head.

The centurion made two further appearances that day. The first when he ordered the man from Cyrene to take the cross and carry it to Golgotha, instead of the Lord. The second appearance was when he stood at the foot of the cross and supervised the Lord's crucifixion.

The Lord stood before them in the Praetorium, savagely beaten and disfigured as He faced into His last steps to Golgotha. Those who saw Him would have wondered at the form of the One who stood before them. Isaiah prophesied that our Lord's face and form would be disfigured more than that of any man (Isa. 52:14).

There they brought the *stauros* (cross) to Him. It was either a stout stake, for that is what the term *"stauros"* means, or as has come down to us through tradition, it could have been a stake with a cross bar. They laid it on His shoulders and faced Him into His first steps of *Via Dolorosa* or the *Via Crucis* (Way of the Cross), winding through the streets of the old city to Golgotha.

Simon of Cyrene

Mark records that there was another man on the streets that day. His name was also Simon, but he had come from Cyrene in Northern Africa. Seeing Simon and watching Jesus' flagging physical strength, the soldiers compelled Simon to pick up the cross and bear the burden (see Mark 15:21). Undoubtedly, the weight of the cross would have been a burden almost more than His shredded shoulders could bear. It was therefore an unexpected mercy, intended or unintended we do not know, when after a few paces from the Praetorium the centurion compelled a man coming in from the country to carry it for Him.

We know so little about this person Mark referred to as Simon of Cyrene and whom he knew as the father of Alexander and Rufus. Cyrene, now a vast ruin, was at that time a prosperous city on a plateau about fifteen miles from the Mediterranean on the north coast of Africa to the west of the Nile delta. Simon was a member of a notable community of Jews in Cyrene and may have been coming to Jerusalem on business when the soldiers compelled Him to carry the Lord's cross. We know no more about him apart from Mark's brief note.

I do know that Simon carried that cross all the way to Golgotha, and when the soldiers took it from him, I cannot imagine that he then went on about the business that had brought him to Jerusalem. I believe that Simon of Cyrene had heard of Jesus of Nazareth and His words and miracles. It is more likely that the knowledge of Jesus burned within him as he stepped back from the cross, found a place among the crowd, and there watched the Lord die.

Did Simon come to faith? Was he drawn, like the second thief, to find in his heart the desire for the Savior to remember him when He came into His kingdom? And was he thankful that circumstances had brought him to the cross? We can never know. But like Simon, I find that all kinds of life experiences have brought me also to the cross, some of which I have deliberately engineered, some were marked out by the Lord, and some had their origin in the impulses of others. And here at the cross at the beginning of the next part of my journey, I have become part of the purpose the Father has marked out for me. And for that, I am thankful.

The Women Who Followed Him

Soon after Jesus was relieved of His cross, the women who knew Him well crowded around Him weeping and filled with grief because of what was about to overtake their Lord. But He was above pity. Modern images of a suffering and weakened Jesus forever hanging on His cross are at odds with the strength that sustained Him along that way of the cross.

Understanding their grief, the Lord turned their faces to a future of which they had no understanding. Their grief was misplaced and needed to be directed not at the One who would die, but towards their own very uncertain futures. In a few short years, Jerusalem would be besieged, many would starve to death, and those who had borne children would desperately wish they had not. It was then that they would experience the greater suffering.

Those women who came weeping to Jesus on the way to the cross are known to us. His mother was there with her sister; Mary, the wife of Cleopas; and Mary of Magdala, whom we know as Mary Magdalene (see John 19:25). But there were others. Another Mary, the mother of James and Joses, and also Salome had come from Galilee to serve the Lord during those last terrible days (see Mark 15:40, 41). Salome was the wife of Zebedee and the mother of James and John.

The distinction between Jesus' disciples and the women who followed Him is marked. On that night all the disciples fled, though John, after his initial steps away from the Lord, returned to follow closely. The women, when they had learned of their Lord's coming death, had gathered around Him, stayed close to Him during those hours of greatest pain, and were then present in the garden where He had been entombed. The disciples were still dispersed and in fear of their lives. I now must ask myself: which of these groups more closely resembles me and my walk with the Master?

The Women of Jerusalem

"And when they came to a place called Golgotha, that is to say, Place of a Skull, they gave Him sour wine mingled with gall to drink. But when He had tasted it, He would not drink" (Matt. 27:33, 34). This act of mercy, according to ancient authorities, had been arranged by an association of Jewish women and was designed to dull the pain and deaden the consciousness of those being crucified. As Jesus was nailed to the cross, He was offered the drink and perhaps, not knowing what it was, took a first sip. Then understanding what they offered Him, He refused it. He would obey the Father's will in the full dignity and strength of His Person, not dulled by any wine, however well-intentioned. For the purchase of my salvation, He would pay the full price of conscious suffering.

Pilate

"And an inscription also was written over Him in letters of Greek, Latin, and Hebrew: THIS IS THE KING OF THE JEWS" (Luke 23:38). Luke's report is bare, but John adds the Jews' protest that Pilate should not write that He was the King of the Jews, but that he should have inscribed that He said He was the King of the Jews (see John 19:21). Pilate was unresponsive and replied that nothing could change the decision he had made (see John 19:22).

Without knowing the ancient teachings about the Messiah, Pilate had combined the image of the One who would come to be the King of the Jews with the corresponding image of the One who would suffer for the sins of His people.

I had been taught, like so many, to focus on His suffering, for that was what had secured my salvation. For many years I have tended to disregard the Lord as the coming King, who will require all of us to give account before His judgment seat. And in failing to focus on the coming King, I long neglected to prepare myself for His coming.

I am reminded that the gospel includes His forgiveness as well as my repentance, confession, and submission to His present and coming rule. And that is an essential element in what I am learning about taking up His cross and following Him. For all of us who do so, He is both present Savior and coming King.

Four Soldiers

"Then the soldiers, when they had crucified Jesus, took His garments and made four parts, to each soldier a part, and also His tunic. Now the tunic was without seam, woven from the top in one piece. They said therefore among themselves, 'Let us not tear it, but cast lots for it, whose it shall be,' that the Scripture might be fulfilled which says: 'They divided My garments among them, and for My clothing they cast lots.' Therefore the soldiers did these things" (John 19:23, 24).

Coming to the place of crucifixion, the soldiers first stripped off His clothes, and then with the hammer and nails, they fastened Him to the cross bar, nailing Him not through the hands, which would have torn apart under His weight but through the wrists. Then they nailed His feet to the small step on which His weight would rest. And coming to His last, most painful resting place, He looked down at the soldiers who had fastened the Son of Man to the cross and were now gathered round His garments disputing over who would take what as part of the booty.

And seeing them there and recognizing that they were unwitting accomplices in His execution, He earnestly prayed that the Father would forgive those who were ignorant of the true nature of what they were doing (see Luke 23:34). I have to ask whether the Lord had a wider audience in mind when He spoke those words. In one sense all of us are accomplices in His execution, for He would not be there had we not sinned. Certainly, like the soldiers, none of us would have understood the implacable purpose of the Father to fasten all our sins into His blameless body. And hearing those words I am filled with awe that it was for me, and for all of us, that our Savior was hanging there.

There is no more uncaring image in the Scriptures than the image of those four soldiers sitting on the ground at the foot of the cross, the Lord's garments spread between them, and casting lots to determine who would leave with what while the Lord was hanging in pain just above their heads.

If I had been sitting there, I would have been transfixed by what was happening on that middle cross. And John, who was also there and who reported the soldiers' responses to the crucifixion, would have had given his deep and compelling attention to the Person he loved. But these four soldiers had no such feelings for the dying Savior. Perhaps they had seen too many crucifixions. Perhaps their work had taught them to shut out their feelings.

Whatever the reasons for the soldiers' apparent apathy, there is much in that record to prompt me to examine how I view the cross, for I am in danger of that same tired apathy. We Christians have had the cross in our religious inventory for nearly two thousand years. And if the cross fails to inspire awe in me, then how am I with a humble and broken spirit to obey the Lord's command to take up my cross and follow Him (see Ps. 51:17)?

And I face a further danger. If my apathy buries the awe I may experience at the cross and replaces it with the mind-numbing observances of religion, then worship that requires me to prostate myself before His majesty becomes another meaningless artifact of that same religion, and I am no further advanced in my journey towards His kingdom.

Mary and John

"When Jesus therefore saw His mother, and the disciple whom He loved standing by, He said to His mother, 'Woman, behold your son!' Then He said to the disciple, 'Behold your mother!' And from that hour that disciple took her to his own home" (John 19:26, 27).

Just as the soldiers' activities at the foot of the cross express the uncaring attitude of disinterested people, so John's account of the Lord's words to him and His mother take us deep into the opposite. For me, there is no more intimate expression of a relationship in the Scriptures than in Jesus' words.

What brought Mary to the cross will be obvious to almost every mother on earth. She had held this One in her arms as He drew His first breath, and when the shepherds testified to His coming, Mary had hid all those wonderful events in her heart and from time to time pondered their significance (see Luke 2:19). She watched Him grow from childhood into adolescence and then into manhood. And now she watched Him die.

We also note that Joseph's name is absent from the record after Jesus, aged twelve, stayed behind in Jerusalem to talk with the teachers. We have to assume that her husband died before Jesus began His ministry, for there is no mention of Joseph at Jesus' first miracle in Cana. It is correct to assume that for some years Mary would have been supported by Jesus, her eldest son, for as the first born, He would have the responsibility for financial care of His family. And when Jesus made Capernaum the base for His preaching tours, that city also became her home (see John 2:12).

We assume that Mary was with the four brothers when they came to Jesus, thinking He was out of His mind. But we cannot know whether the uncertainties about her Son, that plagued His brothers, would also have troubled Mary and whether she

Friday: The Cross

would have also hidden these things in her heart. If she was true to her motherhood, as we believe she was, she would have been torn by the attitudes and words of her other sons, and had to balance their seeming obvious conclusions about their brother with the good sense that had accepted His words in Jerusalem so long ago, "I must be about My Father's business" (Luke 2:49).

Mary was in Jerusalem when her Son was arrested, and she would have followed all those events and known that He had been condemned to death by crucifixion. I cannot begin to imagine the depths of anguish that wracked her soul during those last days of her Son's life. All the things she had hidden in her heart to be quietly pondered may have flooded back like a wave out of control. And so she came to the place of shame at Golgotha.

John was at the cross because he was the disciple whom Jesus loved. When they arrested Jesus at the entrance of the Garden of Gethsemane, all the disciples, including John, deserted their Lord and fled into the night (see Mark 14:50). But somewhere in the darkness of Jerusalem, John must have paused and wondered what he had done, then turned about, found the One he had deserted, and with Peter, attached himself again to the Lord.

When Jesus was taken into the courtyard of the house of Caiaphas very soon after His arrest, both Peter and John were there (see John 18:15–18). It was from that house, for the second time, that Peter fled into the night. But John followed His Lord to the cross and was standing there close beside Mary when Jesus looking down saw them both.

If John's mother and Mary were sisters, as the Scriptures indicate, then Mary was John's aunt, and their relationship provides a further dimension of the Lord's words to His mother. They would no longer have the past relationship of aunt and nephew, but a new and present relationship of mother and son. In obedience to his Lord, the beloved disciple John took Mary into his own home, and from that moment, she became as his own mother (see John 19:27).

John probably took her home because he wanted to not only obey the instructions of his Lord but also spare Mary the terrible agony of seeing her Son die. Having delivered Mary safely into the care of his servants, John then returned to the cross to witness Jesus' final three hours on the cross.

There is a postscript to this narrative. John eventually made Ephesus his home, and it was from there that he was exiled to the island of Patmos. Visitors to the ruins of the ancient city are shown the tomb of John, but guides also indicate that there is another tomb in Ephesus though it is now lost. John had obeyed the Lord's injunction to the end of his life. The other tomb was of Mary whom John accepted as his mother.

The Two Thieves

"'We indeed [are] justly [condemned], for we receive the due reward for our deeds; but this Man has done nothing wrong.' Then he said to Jesus, 'Lord, remember me when You come into Your kingdom.' And Jesus said to him, 'Assuredly, I say to you, today you will be with Me in Paradise'" (Luke 23:41–43).

I have discovered to my cost that the cross is a place of division. It was there that those who were truly intent on the cross, such as John, Mary, and the other women, were separated from those who do not care, like the soldiers, the crowd, and the Jewish leaders, who jeered at the Lord. But there is also a middle, movable ground between the two extremes, for the cross has the power to move a person from the place of denial to the place of acceptance.

But it must be said that the cross cannot move a person; only the One who hung and died there has that power. This is how it was for the two criminals crucified, one on each side of the Son of Man. The two men began in prison and were condemned for unspecified acts. Once they were found guilty, they were condemned to death by crucifixion.

These two men also began with the same evil capacity to blaspheme the Lord, echoing the words of the crowds and of the leaders of the Jews. The crowds said, "'Aha! You who destroy the temple and built it in three days, save Yourself, and come down from the cross!' Likewise the chief priests also, mocking among themselves with the scribes, said, 'He saved others; Himself He cannot save'" (Mark 15:29–31). But only one of the criminals took up the derisive taunt: "If You are the Christ, save Yourself and us" (Luke 23:39). The other turned His face to his coming Savior and said, "Lord, remember me when You come into Your kingdom" (Luke 23:42).

His words confuse me, for he acknowledged that Jesus had a kingdom and would come into it. How had he learned that? From the crowds? Hardly likely! From rumors about Jesus spreading through the city? Possibly! But the dying criminal would have also read the words nailed above Jesus' head: "This is Jesus, the King of the Jews." And if he read them, something may have come alive in his heart, a fire lit by the Holy Spirit, who was always in attendance on the Lord. And in that moment this criminal knew, without a doubt, that Jesus was a king coming into His kingdom, and He had the power to convey citizenship on him.

The dying criminal was talking about something in the future. The Lord put the request into its proper perspective when He replied, "Assuredly, I say to you, today you will be with Me in Paradise" (Luke 23:43). So this dying criminal moved from one side of the page of history, where he was allied with Satan and his fellow dying criminal, to the other side of the page, where he was allied with the Lord who had saved him.

The One on the cross, even in those hours when life was most under threat, fulfilled the prophecy He delivered to His disciples, "And I, if I am lifted up from the earth, will draw all peoples to Myself" (John 12:32). The dying criminal was the first fruits of our Lord's crucifixion, and the cross would take its assigned place in the history of humankind.

Part Two: It Is Finished

Darkness Over All the Earth

"Now when the sixth hour had come, there was darkness over the whole land until the ninth hour" (Mark 15:33). The final three hours of the Lord's human life was spent in darkness. Not some kind of half light like a preliminary dawn, but total darkness. The Father had shut out the light of the sun over the whole land. And this could refer to the whole land of Israel or the whole earth. The words are ambiguous.

But the darkness was not only physical so that one could not see one's hand in front of one's face. It was a darkness that invaded the Lord's Spirit. And perhaps in the mysteries we dare not enquire too deeply into, the Lord, who was the Light, had ceased to radiate His Person over those around Him because the darkness of death had invaded His own Spirit. In those three hours, the Lord had begun to taste death for every person who would ever live on earth (see Heb. 2:9).

But there was something more about that inner spirit darkness in Jesus. Just as darkness is an absence of light, so the light of God had ceased to illumine our Lord, who was made to be sin for all of us. Darkness replaced the light of God in His beloved Son.

And when spiritual darkness invaded the soul of our Lord, physical darkness covered the land from the sixth to the ninth hour.

The Ninth Hour

We have come to the final moments in our journey to Golgotha. Jesus had been on the cross for six hours, and His final suffering was about to begin. The suffering of His stricken body was past Him now. This suffering was beyond any torment evil could ever devise. Two agonies would combine in the Son of Man, and they would flow together over the hill of time into the vast expanse of eternity. Jesus had to process the agony of sin and the further agony of abandonment. And then the plan of salvation, which was determined before the world began, would be accomplished.

At the ninth hour, a number of things took place on the cross. Jesus uttered three statements, preliminary to the darkness being lifted from the land. And we will examine the meanings of each of these in a tight sequence. The first was directed to His Father, the second was directed to those who looked on at the foot of the cross, and the final statement spoken was to all the inhabitants of heaven itself who would have been watching their Lord die.

"And at the ninth hour Jesus cried out with a loud voice, saying, *'Eloi, Eloi, lama sabachthani?'* which is translated, 'My God, My God, why have You forsaken Me?'" (Mark 15:34).

Darkness over all the land was nearly at an end, for it was the ninth hour otherwise known as 3:00 p.m. Up to that point, Jesus, our Savior, had sustained His life, though He could have given it up unfulfilled. But He was there for only one purpose, and that purpose had not yet been accomplished.

But these two great agonies combined in the Savior. All the sins of humankind, from the most petty to the great sins devised by the masters of evil driven by the prince of evil, were bound into the being of our Lord. Then the Father withdrew Himself from His only Son. Shut off the light that had always illumined their relationship and withdrew His Presence.

At the moment our Lord cried out, "My God, My God, why have You forsaken Me?" There was no answering voice from heaven as there had been in the past. No one proclaiming, "You are My beloved Son; in You I am well pleased" (see Luke 3:22) as Jesus had heard at the Jordan. Nor the same affirmation on the Mount of Transfiguration with an added instruction, "This is My beloved Son, in whom I am well pleased. Hear Him!" (Matt. 17:5).

At the cross the voice of the Father was silent. The Light that had always illumined the Son had been shut off. The greatest departure of all was the love that expressed the essential nature of the Father, which the Son depended on while away from His true home.

There can be no greater desertion than this, for love was the essence of their individual lives and their relationship, but first our Lord had to experience the withdrawal of the Father's love and approval. This is the essence of spiritual death. He had to suffer for all; all the graces of the Father had to be withdrawn from the His Son.

The ancient Israelites had long practiced a sacrifice on behalf of all the people of the house of Israel. A goat was brought to the high priest, who symbolically bound all the sins of the people on the goat. It was then driven into the wilderness to die alone for the sins of those people.

The prophetic image of the scapegoat in ancient Israel points forward to the moment when the sins of the world will be transferred to Satan, and he will be led into the wilderness to wander and die, thanks to the life, suffering, and death of our Lord, who was the sacrifice for all humankind. The sins of all humanity were placed symbolically, not on His head, but actually embedded in His heart, and with this terrible burden and without the Father's comfort, He was sent into the wilderness of pain to die alone. He was not in company of those He knew so well or sustained by those who cared. He was completely alone in the wilderness of His final suffering. And this time, as there had been in the garden, there were no angels to sustain and comfort Him.

No one with a human mind will ever be able to comprehend the enormous pain of the Father's desertion that tore the cry from our Savior's soul: "My God, My God, why have you forsaken Me?"

In the last moments of His life, He cried out for something to drink. The soldiers dipped a sponge that was tied to a stalk of hyssop in vinegar and offered it to Jesus. After He received it, he cried out for the third time: "It is finished!" (John 19:30). And in that terrible moment, He fulfilled all that the Father required of Him and the work the Father had given the Son to do was complete.

The Lord's words were not directed to those who stood around the cross nor to generations yet to follow Him. I believe that there could only be one audience for His final words: His Father, who had directed the life, words, and acts of His only Son, as well as the myriad hosts of heaven for whom He was their Lord and God. And history is the lesser audience.

He cried out, and then, as John reports, "and bowing His head, He gave up His Spirit" (John 19:30). The word John used to describe the Lord's last act, which has been translated "gave up" is *paredoken*. It does not mean "let His spirit go." Rather, it tells us that our Lord willingly committed His Spirit to the care of the Father (see Luke 23:46). And so, our Lord died. His walk to Golgotha was over.

We have no need to draw attention to what then took place on the cross. Our journey to Golgotha is complete. All that was left was the response of the Father. Matthew reports, "Then, behold, the veil of the temple was torn in two from top to bottom; and the earth quaked, and the rocks were split" (Matt. 27:51).

The veil of the temple guarded the way into the Holy of Holies where, in ancient times, the ark of the covenant rested. It was the most sacred place. No one other than the high priests was permitted into that place, and they were only able to bring a sacrifice for the sins of all the people of Israel. Direct access to the most high God was prohibited, but the Lord's death changed all that.

Now everyone had direct access to the Father, not only for the sins of the people but also for his or her own sins. The veil that was torn from top to bottom was sixty feet long, thirty feet wide, and around four inches thick. Contemporary records suggest that it took the strength of three hundred priests to hang the veil over the entrance to the holy of holies. Neither human hand nor some accident of nature, as some suggest, could have torn that veil from top to bottom. Only the hand of God could have done that, which thus makes known that the way into the presence of God was now and forever open to all who come with a penitent heart.

At the time of our Lord's death, an earthquake shook the land, and the rocks of the mountains were split. This again was caused by the hand of God, as was the darkness over the land. The earthquake demonstrated the inviolable link between the kingdom of heaven and the physical earth. Bring pain to one, and the other remonstrates in awful sympathy.

There was an outcome of these events. One man who had walked to Golgotha in front of Jesus bearing the placard, "The King of the Jews," had begun that day as an unrepentant pagan. But on that long walk, he had found space in his heart for compassion. He had Simon of Cyrene carry the cross, and then just as Jesus was about to die, also in compassion, he ordered his soldiers to offer the Lord wine to ease His pain.

Surely something had happened in the heart of that man. I believe the cross and something or Someone else had moved the centurion from his unrepentant state to stand in the same place occupied by the dying thief when he spoke with Jesus. It was not only the centurion but also those standing with him, for Matthew reports that when all those standing around the cross felt the earthquake and saw what had been happening on the cross, they acknowledged that truly Jesus was the Son of God (see Matt. 27:54).

Our journey to Golgotha in the footsteps of our Lord has come to an end. But we can't leave our inquiry there, for there is one further event that set the seal on all that the Lord accomplished on the cross. And for that, we have to wait until the third day, the day of resurrection.

In His Footsteps

During the first three hours of Jesus' crucifixion, I identified with those whose lives, for good and ill, were touched at the cross. I found many images of who I am and who I might be. But when I came to the final three hours, I was stricken silent. During that period there were no more human interactions with the Savior. There were only the cries of the Lord Himself, and the sounds of earth and sky crying out

Friday: The Cross

as though tied to the One who created them. And the earth relinquished its hold on some of its dead, and they were seen walking in the city.

How did I approach those wonders? And how did I find in the shallow resources of human wisdom or in the language of the faith I knew so well, the words that would be sufficient for the task of describing what I saw and experienced there? There was nothing in my human catalogue of wisdom that would suit. So where could I look for suitable words to describe the indescribable?

I have learned through His grace, to look inside myself because the One who died on the middle cross now lives there (see Col 1:27; Gal. 2:20). And with the inner ears of my spirit tuned to His voice, I can be attentive to Him and wait to hear the same still small voice that God used when He communicated with Elijah on Mount Carmel. For this was the only way I could readily learn what it meant to take up my cross and follow Him as I had done from Jericho to Golgotha.

That terrible day I stood in darkness at the foot of the cross, but there was another One there with me. He was inexpressibly tender and compassionate, and He knew all the time what was really taking place on the middle cross. He was filled with the light that dispelled all the darkness of the land, which held sway between the sixth and the ninth hours.

I even knew His name: the Spirit of Christ. I was conscious of Him as the darkness lifted, and turning to Him, I found that He was turning to me as He would continue to do throughout the whole of my life. He would become the One who draws alongside to advise, guide, counsel, and comfort. And with that same gentleness, He encouraged me as He would the others, who would see and speak with the risen Lord during the day of resurrection.

Chapter Fourteen
SUNDAY: He Is Risen

Introduction

At the ninth hour, Jesus cried out with a loud voice, "It is finished." At that moment one part of the work the Father sent His Son to do was indeed finished, but His work was not yet complete. Our Lord had faced death for everyone so that none of us should ever die forever. Humanity would never be free from the fear of death until the resurrection, but through Christ's death, everyone now has the opportunity for eternal life.

Very early in the morning on the first day of the week, the women who had come with Him from Galilee, including Mary Magdalene, Joanna, and Mary the mother of James, went to the tomb. Luke reports that when the women came to the tomb and saw the stone rolled away they went in and found that the Lord's body was not there (see Luke 24:2, 3).

I can only wonder at their dismay tempered by astonishment. Luke reports that they were greatly perplexed. Standing in front of the tomb, their perplexity was deepened with fear when two men in white stood before them with a question, "Why do you seek the living among the dead? He is not here, but is risen" (Luke 24:5, 6).

These women were the first witnesses to His resurrection, but all they had seen and heard was an empty tomb and the words of angelic messengers. They then left the tomb, went back into the city, and reported what they had witnessed to the disciples. And being still bowed down with grief the disciples thought the women's words were merely idle gossip, not worth believing. How wrong they were (see Luke 24:11).

Even though their Lord had told them that He would rise again, they were still in a state of desertion. They had not yet embraced the promise that He would rise again. Their fear had overridden the promise that was lodged in their minds but not in their hearts. Only their experience of His resurrection could change that.

The Scriptures contain records of a number of men and women who encountered the living Lord after His resurrection. One woman, two men, and then the disciples themselves without Thomas and then again with Thomas all had some encounter with the Lord. Luke records that the Lord also appeared to Simon Peter, but there are no records that reveal the circumstances of that encounter.

Mary Magdalene

She came out of a tangled past. Somewhere in Galilee she had been exposed to demons and seven of them had invaded her body. The Scriptures have drawn a veil of silence over these circumstances, but she certainly suffered from their invasion as seven personalities competed with her own for prominence. We do not know how old she was when that invasion took place, but her suffering was confronted by the compassionate One she came to know as Jesus of Nazareth, who was a Galileean like her. She is known to us today as Mary Magdalene or Mary of Magdala.

Much of Jesus' ministry took place in Galilee, as He ranged far and wide from His base in Capernaum. Magdala, a little way south of Capernaum and on the west coast of the Sea of Galilee, was famous for its dye works and for the sale of doves necessary in temple worship, and it was most certainly in the Savior's itinerary during one of His teaching journeys. There He encountered Mary with her seven demons and cast them out of her.

Mary Magdalene was one of the women who followed Jesus from Galilee to Jerusalem and made provision for His needs out of their own resources. These women were in the holy city at the time of His arrest and would have quickly learned of the verdict that the One they loved, served, and followed was to be crucified. One can only wonder at their desperate grief when they learned of His coming death and the manner of it. I believe that from that moment, and unlike the disciples who fled, the women kept close watch on what was happening to the beloved Lord.

In the description of events at the cross and then at the garden tomb, Mary Magdalene was always present with one or more of the women who followed Jesus. In this document I have focused only on her so that I can better understand this one who was the first to experience the full wonder of the resurrection.

Matthew reports that Mary Magdalene was standing a little way from the cross watching, as He was nailed through His wrists to the cross bar and through His feet to the peg of wood that would bear some of His weight. She remained watching the cross through the darkness that covered the land from the sixth to the ninth hour. She was there when her Lord cried out, "It is finished," and she watched His body slump in death.

At that point the crowd began to disperse, having had their blood lust and the mob anger that possessed them satisfied, but not Mary Magdalene. She watched as Joseph of Arimathea and Nicodemus came to the cross, drew out the nails from His wrists and feet and carried their Lord's body to a private place where they washed Him and with a hundred pounds of ointment of alum and myrrh, anointed Him for burial then wrapped Him in a linen cloth.

Mary Magdalene followed the two men to the new tomb in the garden, which Joseph had cut for himself, and laid His body on the stone bier against one wall. They then rolled a great stone against the opening and left the tomb, but Mary did not. She and another of the women sat opposite the tomb and kept watch until the sunset and the Sabbath had begun. They then went to the home of one of the women and prepared spices for their own anointing of His body.

It is impossible to plumb the depths of Mary Magdalene's grief and the sense of loss, which was a great emptiness in her soul. Gone were all the tender recollections of the times she had shared with her Redeemer, beginning with the freedom from the spirits that had infested her soul with their venom. Gone were all the delights of providing for His needs from her own purse, and the wonder at seeing Him touch the lame and blind and deaf and heal them. There was nothing left but the pain of His death and the silence of her watch against the tomb.

The next day was the Sabbath, and there are no records of Mary Magdalene's actions on that day of rest. Perhaps she returned to the tomb and continued her watch. Perhaps she hid her grief in the quiet of the house where she was staying

Very early the next morning, the first day of the week, Mary Magdalene and the others went to the tomb wondering how they might roll away the stone. But it had already been rolled away, and when they went into it, they found the tomb empty. Luke continues the account. "And it happened, as they were greatly perplexed about this, that behold, two [angels] stood by them in shining garments. Then, as they were afraid and bowed their faces to the earth, [the angels] said to them, 'Why do you seek the living among the dead? He is not here, but is risen!'" (Luke 24:4–6).

The first glimpse of her Lord's resurrection dawned on Mary Magdalene, but even with the angels' pronouncement and their reminder that He Himself had said that He would rise again, she did not truly believe. It was like a false dawn. There was the promise of resurrection but it had yet to light up her heart. Even so, she and the women went to the apostles and told them everything they had seen and heard. But as we know, the disciples did not believe them.

There is a brief interlude in Mary' story. After the apostles had heard of the empty tomb, Peter and John ran to the tomb, and Peter, entering, saw the linen cloths lying there. We don't know the effect these sights had on Peter, but John, writing many years later, testified, "Then the other disciple, who came to the tomb first, went in also; and he saw and believed" (John 20:8). John reports, "Then the disciples went away again to their own homes" (John 20:10). But Mary, who was a witness to these events, stayed at the tomb.

It was still twilight for her, for neither the words of the angels nor their reminder that Jesus had told them He would rise again, had enough power to dispel the vestiges of darkness and grief in her soul.

She stood outside the tomb weeping, and in her tears she looked into the tomb. There she saw two angels sitting, one where His head had been, the other at His feet. They asked her why she was weeping, and she, in her sadness, confessed that someone had taken away her Lord and she didn't know where to look for Him (see John 20:12, 13). Even the presence of angels could not dispel the darkness that accompanied His death.

At that moment she became aware of a person standing close to her. She did not recognize Him, and she thought that He was the gardener. He spoke to her in that unmistakable voice, "Woman, why are you weeping?" But even His voice, did not dispel her grief. "Sir, if You have carried Him away, tell me where You have laid Him, and I will take Him away" (John 20:15). And still His resurrection had not made itself real to her troubled soul. The possibility of hope eluded her; it was shut away from her heart because she believed that this Man was only the gardener.

He spoke her name, and in that instant everything changed. "Mary!" (John 20:16). And where before there was that inhibiting twilight of unbelief, now the full light of His resurrection dawned on her and she cried out, "Rabboni! (which is to say, Teacher)" (John 20:16). All her doubts fled away. Now she knew that He was alive, and the resurrection had come at last to Mary of Magdala.

Our Hearts Burned Within Us

They left behind a community in disarray. In spite of the report of John, who believed, and Mary of Magdala, who had seen the Lord, most of those in the prototype Christian community in Jerusalem didn't know what to believe. And this confusion was evident to the One who joined the two men on the road to Emmaus. He read it in their voices and on the grief that their faces so evidently betrayed.

The historian in me wants to know the identities of these two men. One of the men was identified by Luke as Cleopas. The other is unnamed, but there are two traditions we can examine in this situation. One very ancient tradition gives the name Simon to this second disciple and declares that both were members of the seventy

Jesus sent out. Another authority (Alfred Edersheim) identifies him with the author of the gospel, which bears his name, Luke.

If the first tradition is accurate, then both these men walking the Emmaus road would have known the voice of the Savior. But the Lord had restrained their understanding so that they didn't know the One who walked and spoke with them (see Luke 24:16). The Greek text reveals that another power had authority over their inner eyes. He had restrained them from that personal knowledge of Himself, and it overrode any memories of His voice that they may have had from previous contacts.

He asked them the topic of their conversation and the reason for their sadness (see Luke 24:17). And they recounted all that they knew about His crucifixion, and all that they had learned from the other disciples, who had heard one thing and believed another. He was alive, yet they had only the words of one woman and the two who had ventured into the empty tomb. In their opinion it was not enough for certain faith.

Then He spoke with them: "'O foolish ones, and slow of heart to believe in all that the prophets have spoken! Ought not the Christ to have suffered these things and to enter into His glory?' And beginning at Moses and all the Prophets, He expounded to them in all the Scriptures the things concerning Himself" (Luke 24:25–27).

And even with this personal exposition, they still did not recognize Him.

So speaking together, or rather listening to the One who spoke of Himself, they arrived at their destination and prevailed upon Him to come in and eat with them, so He did. Then, when He was at the table with them, He took the piece of bread, spoke the blessing, broke it, and gave it to them. In that act He would most certainly have gained their attention, for it was contrary to accepted custom. The guest never broke bread and offered the blessing. That belonged to the head of the house, who presided over the meal.

Luke reports that their eyes were then opened, and they recognized their Lord, and He vanished from their sight. Resurrection had come to that house in Emmaus but only when the obstacles to their recognizing Him had been removed. The sound of His voice, the inner warmth as He expounded the Scriptures, and then their acceptance that He was the Master at that meal as He had been in so many before that time. All this should have alerted them to His presence, but someone had put a blanket over their eyes, both inner and outer, so that the full glory of the resurrection could not dawn upon them until He was ready to reveal Himself. And when He was ready, they had been prepared to receive that revelation of their risen Lord.

So it had been for Mary Magdalene in the garden. There the sound of His voice calling her name was the trigger for the dawning of resurrection. Here, it was the breaking of bread building on what they had already experienced on the road to Emmaus.

Resurrection: the fact that our Lord had overcome death and brought a totally new kind of life to humankind. For Mary and these two men, resurrection was only revealed when the Lord had established the grounds for that revelation. It is presumptuous to believe that revelation is there on demand. And this would be true for the third person in our study: the one people have, without justification, called Doubting Thomas.

My Lord and My God

The two disciples at Emmaus left their meal and hurried back to Jerusalem with the news that they had seen the Lord and had spoken with Him. When they got there, the doors were locked and when the doors had been opened to them, they told the disciples all that the Lord had done. Thomas was absent.

What followed next differs according to different gospels. Both Matthew and Mark omit any record of the Lord's meeting with the disciples in that room on the evening of the first day of the week. Luke writes of only one meeting and telescopes other events into a single record, passing from the meeting of the Lord with the disciples to His ascension. Only John records Jesus' meeting with His disciples with Thomas absent and then with Thomas present.

As soon as the two men from Emmaus had told the disciples of their encounter with the risen Lord, He also appeared among them, for He knew they were still troubled. (Luke reports that they were terrified and frightened.) And in His tender compassion and understanding, He showed them the wounds in His hands, side, and feet. They knew it was their Lord and that He was real, but their joy and wonder were mixed with some residual unbelief (see Luke 24:41). Knowing this, the Lord took some of their bread and ate it, which showed them that His was indeed a living body and that His resurrection was also real. Thomas was absent.

When Thomas returned to their company, they told him that they had seen the Lord. John records Thomas' response, "Unless I see in His hands the print of the nails, and put my finger into the print of the nails, and put my hand into His side, I will not believe" (John 20:25). These are not the words of a doubter being in two minds about something so essential to His future. The Greek word defines doubt as simply that, being in two minds, being faced with two paths or two choices and faltering between the two, as Peter did on the waves when Jesus called Him to come. The words of Thomas were those of a man certain of what He needed: proof that His Lord was indeed alive.

And there is another word Thomas used that is important to all those who long for a resurrection. Thomas told his fellow disciples that he would not believe. The word is best translated as Thomas saying that he would not place his unreserved and unconditional trust with his surrender to the Lordship of the risen Christ until he saw the evidence. This was no muddle-headed man, but one who saw the issue clearly and was prepared to state his case. The resurrection had to be based on evidence.

For Mary, it was the sound of her name. For the two men on the road to Emmaus, it was the revelation of their Master breaking bread. For Thomas, the resurrection could only become real for him when he saw the nail prints and the wound in his Savior's side.

A week later Thomas was again with the disciples, though this time, believing the danger for the Jews had passed, the room was unlocked. Jesus again stood among them, and being true to the same nature that prompted Him to call Mary by her name and to break bread with the two men at Emmaus, He knew exactly what Thomas needed. He stood before His disciple and said, "'Reach your finger here, and look at My hands; and reach your hand here, and put it into My side. Do not be unbelieving, but believing.' And Thomas answered and said to Him, 'My Lord and my God!'" (John 20:27, 28). I can imagine Thomas falling at the Lord's feet in adoration and wonder and declaring his own acceptance of the resurrection of his Savior.

There is a postscript to our Lord's words that reaches across the centuries and seeks to be planted by His Spirit in our hearts with all the force of the Lord's authority. He said to Thomas, "because you have seen Me, you have believed. Blessed are those who have not seen and yet have believed" (John 20:29). The words "have believed" refers to those who have placed their unreserved and unconditional trust in the risen Savior accompanied by their surrender to His Lordship.

In His Footsteps

I walked in the garden where Joseph of Arimathea had cut his tomb, and I watched the unfolding drama around that centerpiece of grief. The servants of Pilate had come and placed their seal across the stone and departed, as though asserting that the puny exercise of human authority could stand against the authority of the Most High God.

I was there when the earthquake shook the garden and the walls of His tomb, as if to say that nothing could forbid the life that would come with His resurrection. And with the earthquake, the angel came and scorning the stone's weight and the authority of the seal, he rolled away the stone and sat on it (see Matt. 28:1, 2).

I watched as the women, still overcome with grief, came with their own spices for His anointing. Finding the great stone rolled away, they went in and found two angels sitting in the tomb. One was at the place where His head had been, and the other was at His feet. They heard the words of resurrection, and with hearts full of hope and rejoicing, they ran and told the disciples. But the disciple's own rejoicing was mixed with unbelief, for they thought that the women were indulged in idle gossip.

Then Mary of Magdala, still believing that death was inevitable, came alone to the tomb, and her encounter with her Lord has already been told. She heard Him speak her name, and at last, His resurrection became real. Then her fear of death, which had bound her for so many years, began to unravel.

Then I recalled what one disciple had written barely forty years after those events. "Inasmuch then as the children have partaken of flesh and blood, He Himself likewise shared in the same, that through [His] death He might destroy him who had the power of death, that is, the devil, and release those who through fear of death were all their lifetime subject to bondage" (Heb. 2:14, 15).

That morning I reminded myself that the word translated "destroy" is *katargeo*, which could also be translated "to render inactive and idle, to spoil, to make useless and void, abolish, make of none effect" (Bullinger, p. 220). The subject of the writer's pen was, of course, the adversary, who was robbed of His power to subdue the people of the world and subject them to fear through the Lord's death on the cross and His subsequent resurrection.

Then I rejoiced in the garden, for my Lord's resurrection had removed from my own heart the possibility of that fear and all its attendant vices. But I heard Him speak a caution into my inner ears. The adversary was indeed powerless, but I could give him back that power every time I thoughtlessly indulged in the works of the world and of the flesh.

I took away from those experiences in Jerusalem, at Golgotha, and in the resurrection garden the humbling understanding that it was in my power to render the cross and His resurrection of no effect. I could strip it of its power.

The weapons that enabled me to render inactive the power of the cross were readily available. I had been born with them: my propensities to fear, the ease with which I entertained unbelief, my familiarity with anxiety, my indulgence in self-centeredness and self pleasing, letting my heart be ruled by my own self-pity, welcoming unrestrained anger into my heart, and so much more. My sinful flesh is well equipped to render the cross and His resurrection ineffective, but only if I submit to the adversary's deceitful rule. But there was another way for those of us, who through His Spirit, would engage the power of His risen life.

I faced into the days ahead with the sure conviction that I had to live in and under the power that His cross and resurrection released into the world. To do that, I had to accept one of the Lord's most demanding invitations; "If anyone desires to come after Me, let him deny himself, and take up his cross daily, and follow Me" (Luke 9:23). And so I shall, for that is why I came to Golgotha.

Chapter Fifteen
Epilogue: Take Up Your Cross

My journey to Golgotha in the footsteps of my Savior is complete. His death on the cross and His conquest of death with all its pains has been fulfilled by His resurrection, and like Thomas, I can fall at His feet and confess, "My Lord and my God." But in another sense my journey with the risen Lord has barely begun.

There is so much of what I have learned on this journey that needs to find a permanent place in my head and heart—particularly in my heart. I now face the challenge of understanding how to live out what it means to take up my cross and follow Him. I have heard His voice like the disciples on the road to Emmaus. I have never heard Him call my name as Mary of Magdala did, though I know that He knew my name before the world began. And I know that I am included in the roll call of the blessed, which is filled with those who have believed but have never seen Him.

What is there left to learn? So much! I have learned, with His disciples, that my path involves me becoming like my Teacher (see Matt. 10:25)—I truly wish to apply His words to my own life. And because I acknowledge myself as both His disciple and His servant, I have to look for patterns embedded in the Scriptures on which I can model myself. And He, my Teacher and Master, is clear about the subject of my search. He is the model for the whole of my life. It is enough for me that I aspire to be like my Teacher and Master.

And that brings me back to His crucifixion, to His resurrection, to what He suffered, to the eternal life that always overcomes death, and to His instruction to all those who would be His disciples. Luke records one of Jesus' instructions that establishes the pattern for my own life as His disciple and bond slave. Jesus told His disciples, "If anyone desires to come after Me, let him deny himself, and take up his cross daily, and follow me" (Luke 9:23).

I took the Lord seriously when I accepted His invitation to invite Him to come into my heart so many years ago. And from that invitation and because of His coming,

His peace as well as the greatest of joy I have ever experienced have found a lodging place in my heart. Although I had not yet plumbed the depths of what He had done for me and what the cross meant, I knew that He was real and that He had a central place in my life.

That central place is explained by Paul in his first letter to the church at Corinth where the apostle wrote, "Do you not know that your body is the temple of the Holy Spirit who is in you, whom you have from God, and you are not your own? For you were bought at a price; therefore glorify God in your body and in your spirit, which are God's" (1 Cor. 6:19, 20).

But in applying the teaching in this passage to my own life, I first have to correct some common mistakes in its interpretation. The personal pronoun translated "you" is plural, as is "bought at a price." However, the terms "body," "temple," and "spirit" are all singular. Paul is referring to the *ekklesia*, which he identified as the body of Christ and the temple of the Holy Spirit. And I, as one of the members of His eternal family, am indissolubly part of the eternal mystery of the cross. For I am one of the living stones in the wall of that temple (see 1 Peter 2:5) and a member of the body of which He is the Head (see Rom. 12:4, 5). Like the church itself, I also am bought at a price, so I belong entirely to Him. My body is His, my mind belongs to Him, and my spirit is linked indissolubly with Him through His own Holy Spirit.

On that central cross at Golgotha, He paid the ransom for my soul with His own life. I must now turn again to Him as I did when I first believed and seek the meaning of what it means to take up my own cross daily and follow Him.

These are the questions I have to address as I learn to carry that cross until my entry into the eternal. Some of the principles I need are drawn from my study of what happened on the cross while what else I need I can find within the writings of that master of the spiritual life, the apostle Paul. And there are seven marks in the Scriptures of what it means to bear my cross:

- I have been crucified with Christ
- Become obedient unto death
- Deny yourself daily
- Follow Him
- The world has been crucified to me
- Not my will but Yours be done
- Resurrection

Each of these seven principles of bearing my own cross demands my careful, undivided, and continued attention.

I Have Been Crucified With Christ

Paul's words to the disciples in Galatia are not merely tidy and intriguing doctrines. They are the heart and pivot of my life as His disciple and the core of what it means to take up my cross and follow Him. The Scriptures are clear. I was crucified in absentia on that central cross. But I need to ask: who was the person crucified with Christ at that time?

The Scriptures are also clear if I can bear to accept them. I am not merely a person burdened with a catalogue of past sins beyond counting. I am also a person who inherited from my parents and beyond them, from humankind's two ancestors in the garden of Eden, a nature that has always been predisposed to sin and independence from my God. I wake up with those tendencies every day of my life and always will, though I cannot and do not find glory in that evil predisposition.

I was also nailed to that central cross and there mercifully died with Him. I am shamed by the fact that He took my sinful nature into Himself and died to strip that sinful nature of its power to rule my life. That part of me was crucified with my Lord and Christ.

The outcomes of that crucifixion cannot be measured. Paul, in the same letter, allows me to know what I inherited when I was crucified with Him. He wrote, "I have been crucified with Christ; it is no longer I who live, but Christ lives in me; and the life which I now live in the flesh I live by faith in the Son of God, who loved me and gave Himself for me" (Gal. 2:20).

This is how eternity becomes part of me. His life, which has no beginning and no end, has been planted within the inner ground of my spirit. And it is within me that my Lord can now express Himself. No longer in words and actions to the men and women He met on the roads of Galilee, Judea, and Samaria, but in the inner confines of my heart in the same gentle, and sometimes not so gentle, voice He used then. He never changes, and I can count on the same tender compassion as He acknowledges my struggles, rebukes me, and instructs me in the ways I should go.

You may ask how does He express Himself within me? In the same way any person expresses themselves when he or she comes into my house. Each one brings a presence into the house that can be read whether it is anger, stress, delight, frustration, self-pity, or the aggravation of being misunderstood. They express themselves in my house, and I read that expression.

In the same way, my Lord expresses Himself to me through two great attributes of His character: His peace (see John 14:27) and His joy (see John 15:11). In the wonder of the early days of my relationship with Him, His peace and joy were my constant companions. I experienced His peace as a great inner sense of well-being. His joy was a song that filled my heart, and both these expressions of His character have been my constant companions. I must confess though that I have often had to work hard to keep my heart safe from distractions so that He can express Himself there.

When I permit other sounds and voices to fill my heart and the disturbances of this world to distract me from loving Him, He withdraws these expressions of His being. He is missing from my heart, and His song is silent until I have restored my own heart to the place of rest where He can express Himself

The cross was a place of cursing, but the Father has turned that place of cursing into a place of blessing. And taking up my cross puts the obligation squarely on my shoulders to understand and make the blessings of the cross part of my daily life. His peace and joy are some of the blessings He has bestowed on me, but there is much more that the cross has made possible for all of us.

We have a negative saying, "He has a mind of his own." And while that is true of independent people who refuse instruction, it is also true of the One who has come to dwell within me. Paul put it this way. "For 'who has known the mind of the Lord that he may instruct Him?' But we have the mind of Christ" (1 Cor. 2:16). Of course! Since He lives within me, He must also think within me. It is worth noting that the term translated "mind" is *nous*, and it incorporates into its broad meaning three quite specific mental activities, which being true of each of us, are also true of the Lord within me.

The first of these elements of the mind of Christ is *noema,* the product of what His mind does, the outcomes of His reflection, what He thinks out. It expresses the thoughts of our Lord dwelling within each of us.

The second elements of the mind of Christ is *ennoia*, which refers to what the mind of our Lord contains. In other words, this element expresses the Lord's ideas, notions, thoughts, intents, purposes, which like Himself are infinite.

The third element of His mind is *dianoia*, which refers to how the Lord thinks through a situation, His capacity to reflect on situations, both my own and everyone else's situations from around the world. Nothing is missed by our Lord's reflective capacities.

And the wonder of it all is that He does all these things within my spirit, enlightening my heart and mind as He chooses, in order to further His purposes for His people and for the world. This inner mental capacity of our Lord was what Paul described in his first letter to the church at Corinth. He described them as gifts, which are also known as the manifestations of His Spirit. Three of those manifestations flow out of my Lord's knowing. The first is the word of knowledge, the second is the word of wisdom, and the third is prophecy (see 1 Cor. 12:8, 10). Each of these is a small fragment of what the Lord knows and shares with His church through the agency of His Spirit.

To deny these manifestations of His Spirit is to deny the benefits and blessings of the cross. In taking up my cross, I take up also the obligation to understand the blessings that the cross made possible, as well as the obligation to remove those mental obstacles that stop Him from expressing Himself within me (see Rom. 12:1, 2).

Become Obedient Unto Death

Why did our Lord submit to the Jewish authorities who wanted to kill Him? Or to ask the same question in a different way: did He have any say in the process that led to His death?

Paul takes us deep into the forces that made the cross the centerpiece of human history. He wrote, "And being found in appearance as a man, He humbled Himself and became obedient to the point of death, even the death of the cross" (Phil. 2:8). The deeper meaning of that process is embedded in the word "obedient." It is the Greek word *hupekoos,* which refers to the Lord listening attentively to the One issuing the command, in this case the Father. Or to state the same principle another way, the Lord's attentive listening defined the pathway for the Father's instructions. Without the Lord's careful listening, there could be no instructions from the Father and hence no obedience unto death.

When I apply this principle to myself, I learn that obedience, which follows my careful listening to the Lord's personal instructions, bypasses the idea of obedience to a doctrinal injunction or to an order based on religious authority.

His obedience unto death required two things. The first element was a relationship of perfect trust flowing out of an open heart, between the One directing, in this case the Father, and the One being directed—the Lord. The second element in obedience unto death is the ability of the Lord to be listening attentively to the instructions from the Father. Neither the Jewish leaders nor Pontius Pilate nor the crowd had anything to do with it.

When I transpose these matters into our times, I find that this kind of obedience is intimately bound up with me taking up my cross and following Him. At issue are the twin questions: do I enjoy an intimate relationship with my Lord? And do I have attentive inner ears to listen and discover what He requires of me?

I see this kind of obedience in the service of many in the early church. Ananias in Damascus knew how to listen and hear the Lord's instructions, and even though what the Lord told him to do offended his sense of what was proper, he obeyed and sought out Paul, who had been led blind into the house from the Damascus road (see Acts 9:10–18).

Peter and John knew the cost of taking up their cross and following the Lord. The chief priest and some of the Sadducees had put them in prison. However, the Lord had further plans for His servants, so an angel of the Lord opened the prison doors that night. He gave them instructions that would have run counter to what could have been called "good sense." "'Go, stand in the temple and speak to the people all the words of this life.' And when they heard that, they entered the temple early in the morning and taught" (Acts 5:20, 21). In other words, the Lord asked them to put themselves back in the place of danger.

In both cases, the obedience of Ananias and then of Peter and John, required attentive inner ears that could hear and interpret. They could then obey the Lord's instructions even though they seemed to run counter to human wisdom. And this marks out one of the costs for me of taking up my cross and following Him.

Do I have a choice? Of course! Though the choice may be costly and may even lead to death. Just before His ascension, the Lord had told them, "But you shall receive power when the Holy Spirit has come upon you; and you shall be witnesses to Me in Jerusalem, and in all Judea and Samaria, and to the end of the earth" (Acts 1:8). It is a fact of history that all of the apostles except John died because of their obedience, fulfilling the pattern their Lord had set. The Greek word translated "witness" is the word *marturia*, and it is where we get the English word "martyr." That word is a testimony of all those in the first century and beyond who were all obedient to the voice of the Lord unto death.

Obedience to the Lord's direct commands and instructions is not something we argue about. There are no qualifications we can impose, or dare impose, on His instructions. We cannot say, "Yes, I will obey, but ...." It is a salutary lesson for each of us to apply Paul's words to the disciples in Corinth when he defined the divinely appointed personal environment for obedience. "Do you not know that ... you are not your own? For you were bought at a price; therefore glorify God in your body and in your spirit, which are God's" (1 Cor. 6:19, 20). I have to conclude that my obedience until death is not a spare item in my Christian agenda. It is a divinely appointed obligation.

Deny Yourself Daily

The Greek word translated "deny" is very radical. It does not refer to a passing whim of denial like refusing to buy chocolate because it will increase my weight or denying myself the pleasure of sleeping in just this once. The Greek word is *aparneomai*. It means to completely and utterly deny myself, not just once, but as a continuing way of life, without leaving a crack in the armor through which my own will can get out and do its own thing. And when there are occasional cracks, my commitment to deny myself as a way of life seals them up quickly.

Bearing His cross was a full-time event for the Son of the Father, and it culminated in His terrible cry for the Father to take the cup of inexpressible suffering from Him, but only if it was the Father's will to do so. The Lord then acknowledged that the Father's will, not His own, was the guiding principle in His life (see Luke 22:42). That is denial of the first order. And in that moment He acknowledged, as He had throughout His life, that His life wasn't His own, for it belonged to His Father to direct as He willed. This lesson had been learned very early in His life and was expressed when He told His mother, in the form of a question, that he had to be about His Father's business (see Luke 2:49).

In taking up this standard for bearing my own cross, I have to ask the critical question: what does it mean to deny myself? The answer to that question hinges on the answer to another. Who am I? And what part of my complex being am I to deny? Not my mind, although what I know and how I think has been corrupted by my lifelong engagement in the ways of the world and my entanglement in the ways of sin. Not my body, which He created and must be kept in a state where it can carry me to wherever He wants me to go. Not my spirit, for that has been renewed and because of its renewal, has become fit to be in union with the Holy One of God, His own Spirit, which is the Spirit of Christ.

But there is one element of my being that would like me to pass by and ignore its existence. That essential part of me is, and has always been, antagonistic to the claims of my God. It likes to hide in the shadows and pretend it has nothing to do with all the wrongdoing I am predisposed to do. It likes to deny that it is the source of my sin and the stimulus of my stubborn words and thoughts and my acts of independence against my God.

Paul gave it a number of names, but the most telling identity of all was "the flesh." And this has to be the focus for my lifelong commitment to deny myself so that I can fulfill His instruction to take up my cross and follow Him.

Paul described the flesh as having a number of characteristics, but the most critical was what he described in his letter to the disciples in Galatia when he taught them about the great battle we must all fight of our human desires against God's Spirit (see Gal. 5:17). The Greek word translated "lusts" is another extreme word. It is *epithumeo,* which can also be translated as the desire that attaches itself to some object, experience, or person and thus becomes locked in that attachment, for the will of the flesh will not let the desire go and desire will not let the will go.

When I think my desire for something is apparently satisfied, it still will not let my will go. My desire remains permanently dissatisfied. Its satisfaction is always temporary for desire is a never-ending cycle that drives all human life, word, and action, in the human flesh and in the world. Desire is one of the weak and beggarly elements on which the world has been constructed (see Gal. 4:9).

I know as so many have before me that taking up my cross and denying the flesh cannot be achieved in the energies of the flesh. Taking up my cross cannot be done, as the old hermits did, by renouncing the flesh and going to live in a cave or on the top of a pillar, or by beating my flesh into submission. Renouncing the flesh with these kinds of abstentions cannot get rid of its weaknesses. It merely forces it into some kind of temporary submission from which it will soon break out, for that is the nature of my aggressive and irascible old nature.

Paul instructs all of us in two principles as we learn how to take up our cross. The first is an echo of the cross itself. Paul teaches us that those who belong to our Lord have to crucify the flesh with all its contrary passions and desires (see Gal. 5:24). Put it to death. Put off all the works of the flesh. But that is only part of the way of victory over your old self.

In the same letter, Paul adds the second part, "I say then: Walk in the Spirit, and you shall not fulfill the lust of the flesh" (Gal 5:16). And this is a whole new dimension. For all of us who have grown up in the world of human sensibilities know the world of the Spirit is an alien world. So that confronts me with quite a new challenge.

I have been born by His Spirit into His kingdom, which is a kingdom of Spirit where God, who is Spirit, rules. My challenge, and the greatest challenge I have ever faced, is to learn how to live and walk in that world of Spirit and make it my daily habitat. For that world of Spirit is the only place where I can take up my cross and follow Him.

But I am not alone in meeting that challenge. I have One who walks beside me. My Lord called Him the Comforter, the One who comes alongside me. He was also called the Spirit of Truth, for it is His work throughout all ages that leads all of us into all truth. This includes the truth of the cross and the truth of me taking up my cross, denying myself, and following Him. With that, we are brought to the next part of our study.

Follow Me

The challenge to follow Him as I take up my cross and deny myself daily is not as easy as it sounds. In the Greek text, following Him is patterned after the ancient relationships between student and teacher, bond slave and master, and soldier and commanding officer.

The Greek word translated "follow" is *akoloutheo*, and it was used to describe the three relationships listed above.

That might have been easy for those disciples, who walked with Him along those long and dusty roads so long ago, but His command has to be brought into the twenty-first century and into our world. I do not mean into the world of human sensibilities but instead into the world of spirit, His Spirit and my spirit in union with each other.

The first ones to obey that command were the two pairs of brothers, Peter and Andrew, and James and John. They had been cleaning their nets, which they had drawn up on the beach, so that they could remove the rubbish the nets had collected, and repair the nets' torn and tangled cords (see Luke 5:2; note that Matthew's and Mark's accounts are slightly different). Jesus said to them, "Follow Me, and I will make you fishers of men" (Matt. 4:19). Matthew records their response, "They immediately left their nets and followed Him" (Matt. 4:20).

Matthew's own response to follow Jesus was just as radical. He himself reports in the simplest of words that he got up from his seat and followed the Lord (see Matt. 9:9). What is not reported in either of these records is the cost to the disciples of following their Lord. Peter comes close to revealing that in his response to the Lord that Mark records, "See, we have left all and followed You" (Mark 10:28).

We need to ask: what does "all" include? And how does that apply to you and I in the twenty-first century? For these five disciples, all from Capernaum, they left behind their employment and therefore the certainty of income. These ties had been replaced by the new tie of their relationship with Jesus. In addition, their family obligations were also left behind, and Peter was married. We know nothing of the marriage relationship, if any, of the other disciples. In addition, there would have been a network of friends, which in modern terms we call a support network, which they also left behind.

Jesus was just as radical in His statement about the cost of following Him when He spoke to the multitudes, "If anyone comes to Me and does not hate his father and mother, wife and children, brothers and sisters, yes, and his own life also, he cannot be My disciple" (Luke 14:25, 26). It is true that He was seeking to deter those in the multitude who were looking for an easy discipleship. But there are important principles here that relate also to us across the centuries.

The word for "hate" is *miseo*, and when it is applied to the choice between family members and the Lord, it can also mean "to love less." It does not refer to active hate as an aggressive emotion that can so easily result in violent behavior. Following

Jesus is about making constant choices. In any situation you or I may have to choose between obligations to family and obligation to the Lord. And in every case, following Him and being His disciple means that where He requires it, He always comes before any other relationship.

However, hating myself falls into an entirely different category. He bought me at a price, and my whole life belongs by right of purchase to the One who ransomed my life on the cross. These principles of following Him apply to my moment-by-moment walk with the Master. At any moment I may be faced with the choice between the demands, prompts, and willful desires of my sinful nature on the one hand and the call to live and walk in and be led by His Spirit on the other (see also Rom. 8:11).

Central to this call to follow Him is my willingness to permit His Spirit, who is my Teacher, to have continuing access into my inner being. This way, He can tune and train my inner ears to hear His voice as I walk beside or close behind Him. I must confess, however, that His work in me is complicated by my stubbornness, which so often agrees with some important principle of the spiritual life while at the same time seeks to express my relationship with Him in bad practice.

My problem and the problem for all those who would follow Him is that there are so many voices demanding my attention that can so easily be diverted from the still small voice, which is His chosen means of communication. There are voices coming out of the world, from the opposite sex, from political advertising, or from the shrill voices of fellow Christians demanding that I solve their intransigent and unsolvable problems.

The challenge for me is to learn how to keep these many seductive and discordant voices out of my inner being, isolate them in the outer limits of my brain, and keep the inner place where He dwells secure from their noises. Now that is a challenge worth learning as I follow Him. Hearing His voice in any and all situations has to be my highest priority, for that is why He invites me to walk beside Him or just behind Him and always within the sound of His voice.

The World Has Been Crucified to Me

This is one conflict that has been around since Cain went off to build the city called Enoch (see Gen. 4:17). From that beginning other cities were established and Babylon, the epitome of the world's cities, came into being. With these cities the world was defined, and all the weak and beggarly elements that are the foundation for all the operations of the world came into being.

The Lord was very clear about the relationship between His kingdom and the world that He spoke of in His prayer to the Father, affirming that His disciples did not express the world's values and principles in the same way that He had always set Himself apart from the world (see John 17:16). By inference, the Lord indicated that there are parallel worlds: one where His disciples had been born, and the Spirit world that was His permanent dwelling place. Two kingdoms and two ways of life, two sets of principles that govern the way of life in each kingdom, and two authorities with oversight over their separate kingdoms. The Lord our God reigns over His own kingdom of light, and the prince of darkness rules over all the kingdoms of this world (see Luke 4:5, 6).

One of the tragedies of our times is that so few who own the name of our Lord can tell the difference between the ways of life in the two worlds that Jesus identified, for they are so used to the ways of this world pretending to be ways of the kingdom of our God. And the ways of both kingdoms have become inseparably interwoven into the lives of those who would be the Lord's disciples.

This does not have to be, for the Father made provision on the cross for each of us to deal with the destructive and deceitful practices of the world. Paul explains in a most personal statement of where he stood in his day, "But God forbid that I should boast except in the cross of our Lord Jesus Christ, by whom the world has been crucified to me, and I to the world" (Gal. 6:14). On the cross Jesus accomplished a complete work for me in relation to the world. It was there that I died to the world and the world died to me. Because of the cross, the world no longer has any power over me, unless I choose to give it that power.

I believe that John, the beloved disciple, was present when the Lord prayed this prayer to His Father, for he is the only one who records it. John certainly knew the distinctive characteristics of the two competing and antagonistic worlds when he wrote his first letter. There he began with an instruction and went on to describe what the world is all about. Desires that come into our soul through what we see, desires of the flesh that the world brings alive, and the pride of life sponsored and aggressively supported by the world are not of God (see 1 John 2:16).

It is most important to note that John included the verb *agapao*, which is to love God with His own divine love. This love can be prostituted and misused. John asserts that those who prostitute this divine love and direct it to the most unworthy of objects (the world) will suffer the most aggravated consequences. The Father will withdraw His own love, His *agape* from them.

John's words are an application of the Lord's own injunction, "No servant can serve two masters; for either he will hate the one and love the other, or else he will be loyal to the one and despise the other. You cannot serve God and mammon" (Luke 16:13). It is all a matter of choice.

The cross gives me the power and authority to face the world and see it for what it is. I see now that it is full of deceit and subtle distractions, and I would much rather face into the ways of the kingdom of light and allow His light to become part of my own soul. I have learned that I must take James' words to heart. I cannot face in both directions. In a passage devoted to the distinction between the ways of the world, James asked his readers whether they knew that friendship with the world amounts to enmity with God, instructing sinners and those who are double-minded to draw near to God and submit their lives to Him (see James 4:4, 8).

The cross has another power, for it deprives the world of my allegiance if I choose to face away from all its multitude of temptations. I am dead to the world. There is nothing in me that the world wants because I am a child of the Father. The cross makes me a stranger to the world. Each of the elements of His character, which the Holy Spirit expresses in my renewed spirit (see Gal. 5:22), are despised by the world. People of the world cannot understand the divine values that set the people of God apart from the people of the world. And even though the world attempts to substitute these divine elements of His character with human values, they always fall short.

Taking up my cross means that I must face into what the cross makes possible in my relationship with the world. I have to take these principles and integrate them into my life. I must seek the power to translate these powerful principles into daily practices. In this way I will be insulated from the diverse and quite energetic principles of the world that were quite defeated when the Lord died in my place on the cross.

Not My Will But Yours Be Done

I have learned to be very selective about the cross. Like so many others, I was taught that the cross is the place where the price was paid in full for all my sins and my salvation secured. This is the foundation of my salvation. But I had stopped there. I was once like a man finding a castle on the top of a high hill and there been introduced to the Door Keeper, who invited me to enter. When He told me that my repentance and confession would open the castle doors, I readily agreed because my heart told me I was indeed a sinner who needed to be saved.

On the castle steps, I repented, confessed my sin, discovered that the cross made my forgiveness possible, and I stepped across the threshold into the castle precincts. My salvation was assured, a place in heaven was guaranteed, and I came into the entry hall of that wonderful place. And because I had never been taught otherwise, I found myself staying, quite contentedly in the entry hall. I was locked into the four walls of my first experience of His family of which I had now become a member. I never thought to question whether there was anything more to follow. In that frame of mind, I would never explore the wonders of that vast castle and make them mine. The tragedy is that I discovered later in life that, as a child of the Father, all the delights of that vast environment were mine by right. But only if I exercised that right.

My life as a child of the Father is a little like that, and my understanding of the will of God follows the same tragic pattern. I gain so much compared to my previous life, but what I gain is so little compared what has yet to be gained. The key to walking through every part of that castle and enjoying all its treasures is knowing, understanding, and living under the umbrella of the Father's will.

In the garden the night He was betrayed, the Lord finally dealt with the agony of His soul when taking into His own being all the sins of humankind from the first sin of Adam to the last sin before He calls us home. The will of God for my Lord was as much part of His life as was the air He breathed.

Without the Father's will He would have been a forgotten man. He would have been wise like Socrates, religious like Buddha, competent in argument and discussion, an orator above His times, but unable to walk through death and leave that demon of all humankind forever conquered. But with the will of the Father empowering Him into and through the pain of the cross and through death itself, all things became possible. And so it will be for all of us as we take up the cross and follow Him. But this places all of us squarely in front of questions that have plagued those who believe since Pentecost. What is the will of God? And how are we to know it?

We can immediately set aside the theoretical positions that have been the basis of so much doctrine. It is the will of God that all should be saved. It is His will that we go into all the world and make disciples of all peoples. It is His will that we devote ourselves to the Lord's teachings. And it is His will that Satan be defeated.

None of that is in doubt, but these general statements of what the Lord wants add very little, if anything, to my understanding of the decisions involved in me taking up my cross. These statements are too general. I need something much more specific if I am to obey His instruction to take up my cross daily and follow Him. But where am I to find it? I have to go back to the Scriptures where all things for my instruction have been written.

The Greek word interpreted "will" is *thelema*, which can be understood as, the active intent of the Father, His wish for something to be done, His desire for a particular action which will extend His kingdom and rule. And, as it was with Jesus, making the Father's will known is always progressive. It always functions in the present as it did for the disciples when the jealous rulers of the Jews put them in prison. They were not told that they would be released. Nor were they told how or when the prison doors would be opened for them, if ever. And the Father did not tell them what they were to do in the event that their freedom was secured. Theirs was a progressive revelation of the Father's will.

It will always deal with the here and now, for it is built into the Greek word *akoloutheo*, which is translated "follow." We know that this word applies to the relationships between student and teacher, soldier and commanding officer, and slave and master. In none of these cases does the One commanding the other issue general instructions except as a broad framework for His much more specific commands. They are always specific and directed to the immediate need and situation being addressed.

This was the case when Paul and Silas were on their second missionary journey. They tried to go first into Asia and then into Bithynia, but neither direction was according to the Lord's will. Only when they had finally come to Troas did the Lord reveal through a vision the next element in His will: Macedonia.

It is enough for me that I be as my Teacher and Master. He accepted the restraints of the Father's will for those final hours as I believe He had for the whole of His life. Taking up my cross and following Him means that the same restrains apply. It can no longer be my will that directs my life. Only His will has the ability to be sufficient enough for all the challenges that life will put in my way. And to know His will I must be listening attentively to His voice. This will not be a doctrinaire and general statement of His will like "It is His will that all should be saved." The continuing unfolding of His plan for me in all the contexts of life depends on quite specific directions applicable in specific situations.

To that end I have to continually train my inner ears to be always listening. I must be like a good student listening for the word of the teacher, the soldier listening for orders, and the bond slave listening for what he or she must do in order to please the Master. This is all part of the cost of taking up my cross and following Him.

Resurrection

The cross is incomplete without resurrection. Sin and its companion, death, were faced when He hung on the cross, and their penalties and terrors were forever abolished. No longer would we need to fear the great enemy, as the writer to the Hebrews stated, "Inasmuch then as the children have partaken of flesh and blood, He Himself likewise shared in the same, that through death He might destroy him who had the power of death, that is, the devil, and release those who through fear of death were all their lifetime subject to bondage" (Heb. 2:14, 15).

Taking up my cross to follow Him brings me squarely into the same benefits. The devil was defeated on the cross, though His final judgment will have to wait until the end of the age. Death has been forever shredded of its terrors, and I am no longer in bondage to the fear of death that grips multitudes of the world's people. In its place I inherit the most wonderful gift anyone on earth could ever receive. It is the life of Jesus Himself. I have His life, which impelled Him into confrontation after confrontation and always with Himself emerging the victor. That is the life I received when I passed through the narrow gate following His forgiveness. And this life I received is eternal. So that like Him, I have the same heritage. The death that once reigned in me has been swallowed up in victory (see 1 Cor. 15:54).

The apostle John knew the eternal life that had lived for so many years within his aging frame. He wrote of it in his first letter. "This is the testimony: that God has given us eternal life, and this life is in His Son. He who has the Son has life; he who does not have the Son of God does not have life" (1 John 5:11, 12).

And so I face into a most uncertain future. Plagues, disease, and famine ravage the globe. Earthquakes trigger enormous tsunamis with thousands buried in their devastation. National leaders are under threat from neighbors or from their own people. But I stand secure under the burden of the cross He invited me to bear. And I do not carry it alone, for as Paul taught, I am part of the mystery, the unveiling of a wonder that has been hidden for so long. Paul wrote of "the mystery which has been hidden from ages and from generations, but now has been revealed to His saints. To them God willed to make known what are the riches of the glory of this mystery among the Gentiles: which is Christ in you, the hope of glory" (Col. 1:26, 27).

There is one more charge I receive as I face into the future. This charge turns my focus away from myself. It is through carrying my cross and because of His resurrection that I stand at His side surveying the world of sinners, knowing that I now share that charge with Him. The Father has never been willing that any of His creatures should perish but that, in the grace of God, all have the opportunity to come to the saving place of repentance (see 2 Peter 3:9).

This was the subject of Peter's first statement of the gospel at Pentecost where three of the great themes of the gospel came together: His death and resurrection, their repentance, and the gift of life through the Holy Spirit.

When the crowd responded to Peter's words with the searching question about what they should do to be saved (see Acts 2:37), Peter added the second and third elements in the gospel recorded in this chapter. "Repent, and let every one of you be baptized in the name of Jesus Christ for the remission of sins; and you shall receive the gift of the Holy Spirit" (Acts 2:38).

This gospel was taken by ordinary disciples out of Jerusalem after the martyrdom of Stephen, and Luke reports that those who were scattered went everywhere carrying with them the good news of the gospel of their Lord (see Acts 8:1, 4). The gospel was on the road.

The words "preaching the word" are instructive of how the news of Jesus Christ, His death, and His resurrection were to be taken into all the world. The word Luke used was *euangelizomai*, which is best translated as talking about the Lord and discussing the good news with people they met. The translation "preaching the word" hardly does this Greek word justice and tends to exclude ordinary Christians, such as you and me, from any responsibility for spreading the good news.

Now, with my cross squarely on my shoulders, I have to face away from focusing only on the inner life He has given me and turn to the world of the lost. When I took up my cross, He made me the custodian of the gospel, as He has done with so many before me. The personal meanings of His death and resurrection are mine to bear into those parts of the world where He directs me to go.

By accepting the challenge to take up my cross and follow Him, I accept also this responsibility: to go where He goes, following close beside Him, always within the sound of His voice, and as a slave with his Master, I must listen intently to every one of His instructions so that those who dwell in darkness may receive His light.

And so I face into the future together with all those who bear the same great weight of Jesus Christ. When I come at last to the vast realm of eternity, I will pass effortlessly beyond death and enter into the realm where He has gone before to prepare a place for me and for all of us. My journey to Golgotha and beyond will be forever over, and I will be in the company of my Lord forever.

We invite you to view the complete
selection of titles we publish at:

www.TEACHServices.com

Scan with your mobile
device to go directly
to our website.

Please write or email us your praises, reactions,
or thoughts about this or any other book we publish at:

P.O. Box 954
Ringgold, GA 30736

info@TEACHServices.com

TEACH Services, Inc., titles may be purchased in bulk for
educational, business, fund-raising, or sales promotional use.
For information, please e-mail:

BulkSales@TEACHServices.com

Finally, if you are interested in seeing
your own book in print, please contact us at

publishing@TEACHServices.com

We would be happy to review your manuscript for free.

www.ingramcontent.com/pod-product-compliance
Lightning Source LLC
Chambersburg PA
CBHW081840170426
43199CB00017B/2791